CONTENTS

1
ILL BLOWS THE WIND 7
What's in the Air?
A Growing Problem
Urban Air Quality
Some Controls on Pollution

2
YELLOW SMOG, BROWN HAZE 14
The Chemical Stew
Effects of Smog Ozone
Other Smog Ingredients
Controlling Urban Air Pollutants
New Fuels?
Calls for Expanded Public Transit Systems

3
ACID RAIN 26
How Acid Rain Forms
Measuring Acidity
Acid Rain Effects on Soils and Water
Dying Trees
Effects on Agricultural Crops
The Politics of Acid Rain Controls

4
GLOBAL WARMING 39
The Greenhouse Theory
Why Greenhouse Gases Have Increased
How Warm, How Soon?
Effects of Global Warming
Where's the "White House Effect"?
Cooling It

5
ATTACK ON THE OZONE LAYER 54
What Happens in the Stratosphere?
CFC Research
Expeditions and Observations
Research over the North Pole
Effects of Ozone Depletion
Resistance to Controls
Finding CFC Substitutes

6
POISONS IN THE AIR 67
Toxic Chemical Inventory
Toxic Emissions from Pesticides
Poisonous Emissions from Waste
Citizen Protests
Reducing Hazardous Emissions

7
THE ULTIMATE POLLUTANT 80
Hot Spots of Nuclear Waste
What to Do with Radioactive Waste?
The Nuclear Debate Goes On
How Much Radiation Is "Safe"?

8
HAZARDOUS INDOOR AIR 89
Who's at Risk from Radon?
Cigarette Smoke
Asbestos

AIR POLLUTION

KATHLYN GAY

Franklin Watts
New York • London • Toronto • Sydney
An Impact Book   1991

Diagrams by Vantage Art, Inc.

Photographs copyright ©: Photo Researchers, Inc.: p. 6 (Richard Hansen); Battelle Columbus Laboratories: p. 17; NASA: p. 59; Care Photo: p. 106 (John Everingham); all other photographs courtesy of the author.

Library of Congress Cataloging-in-Publication Data

Gay, Kathlyn.
    Air pollution / Kathlyn Gay.
    p.   cm.—(An Impact book)
    Includes bibliographical references and index.
    Summary: Examines the growing problem of air pollution, its effect on the ozone and stratosphere and what we can do to improve air quality.
    ISBN 0-531-13002-9
    1. Air—Pollution—Juvenile literature.   [1. Air—Pollution.
2. Pollution.] I. Title.
TD883.13.G39   1991
363.73'92—dc20   91-17780 CIP-AC

Copyright © 1991 by Kathlyn Gay
All rights reserved
Printed in the United States of America
6 5 4 3

Lead-Laced Air and Dust
Toxic Household Products
Cleaning Indoor Air

9
CLEAN AIR—HOW DO WE GET IT?   102
Global Concerns
The Population Issue
International Agreements/Programs
Renewable Energy Sources
Energy Efficiency

10
THE BUCK STOPS HERE   114
Saving Energy
Planting/Preserving Trees
Be a "Green" Consumer
Getting Involved

Glossary   124

Source Notes   127

Bibliography   133

Organizations to Contact   139

Index   141

Smoke billowing out of an electric plant in Morro Bay, California, is silhouetted against the setting sun.

1
ILL BLOWS THE WIND

Half the acid rain that falls on eastern Canada originates in the U.S., mostly from coal-burning Midwestern electric utilities. . . . Canadians have become increasingly alarmed about the damage it is doing to their lakes, streams, and forests. . . . Not that the Canadians are exactly Snow White when it comes to air pollution. Some of the dirtiest smokestacks in North America lie [in southern Canada].[1]

Poland's factories and furnaces burn cheap, dirty coal. . . . Its air is so foul with heavy metals that it is dangerous to eat vegetables grown outdoors in some areas. . . . Poles' life expectancy is shortened; their rates of cancer and birth defects are higher than their European neighbors'.[2]

It was difficult to describe the color of the sky. . . . It was not quite gray. . . . After all the years of experts preaching about air pollution,

> *a few hot, gray—or perhaps yellow—days were finally making ordinary Canadians pay attention.*[3]
>
> *The 25,000 member [U.S.] Association of Flight Attendants strongly supported the total ban on airline smoking . . . the Journal of the American Medical Association said that in airliners' nonsmoking sections, the levels of airborne nicotine that flight attendants and passengers are exposed to are equivalent to those found in the smoking section.*[4]
>
> *Up smokestacks, through vents and out windows, U.S. manufacturers released 2.6 billion pounds of toxic pollutants into the air.*[5]

These news stories from sources around the world illustrate the heightened concern about air pollutants. Perhaps William Shakespeare's metaphor of long ago sets the tone for the last decade of the twentieth century: "Ill blows the wind that profits nobody." Today's polluted air certainly benefits no one, except perhaps those who would gain financially from the methods they develop to clean up the atmosphere—the air that surrounds the earth—and the air inside our homes, offices, schools, factories, and other buildings.

WHAT'S IN THE AIR?

When breezes or winds blow, people are aware of the flow and resistance of air. It wafts around us, barely noticeable, since it is colorless, odorless, and tasteless—unless the air is polluted with particles of dust or soot, smoke, pollen, or unpleasant odors.

Normally, dry air is made up of gases, primarily nitrogen (78%) and oxygen (21%), plus trace amounts of other gases, such as argon, ozone, carbon dioxide, and methane. Water vapor, or moisture in the form of a gas, and tiny particles in small amounts usually are present but invisible in air. Natural events such as volcanic eruptions, forest fires touched off by lightning, and dust storms may release so-called contaminants into the air, such as gases and solid particles, or solid particulate matter (SPM), the label used by air quality experts. But over hundreds of billions of years, many of these compounds have become part of the atmosphere.

Air becomes polluted because of human activities. Think of dirty air and you may remember skies darkened with smoke from industries or power plants. Or you might recall inhaling unpleasant odors from chemical manufacturing or vehicle exhaust fumes that hurt your lungs.

Many pollutants in the air, however, cannot be seen or smelled. Some may be a result of industrial activities or use of consumer products. Colorless and odorless gases or tiny particulates may be emitted into the air and combine or react chemically with other substances or gases to create compounds harmful to living things and inanimate objects. Other invisible compounds are part of the environment but sometimes may be harmful to people. Radon gas, for example, occurs naturally as part of the decay process of uranium ore in rocks and soils, but if the gas seeps into a home and is inhaled over a period of time, it can be a health hazard.

A GROWING PROBLEM

When people lived primarily in rural areas, and cities were scarce, air pollution was hardly a concern. Smoke or dust would blow away with the winds or wash away with rain or snow. But the industrial revolution brought with it increasing numbers of factories and large urban populations. As urban areas grew, so did the number of cars, trucks, buses, planes, and a vast number of consumer products that have added pollutants to the atmosphere.

Since the early part of the 1900s, most of the pollutants in urban centers have come from the combustion, or burning, of fossil fuels—those that contain hydrocarbons—primarily high-sulfur coal and oil. When fossil fuels are burned, they produce sulfur dioxide (SO_2) and oxides of nitrogen (NO_x), gases that may combine with moisture in the atmosphere and form acidic substances. Burning fossil fuels also contributes to a pollutant known as smog ozone.

Ozone is a natural part of the environment, but it also forms when sunlight strikes nitrogen oxides, hydrocarbons, and other volatile organic compounds (VOCs), which are highly reactive, or changeable, gases. These gases come from a variety of industries, vehicle exhausts, and consumer products. As the nitrogen oxides and VOCs "stew" in the sun, the reaction that takes place produces ozone, the main ingredient in smog.

Other air pollutants include carbon monoxide (CO), which results from incomplete combustion or burning fuels in areas with low levels of oxygen, such as in motor vehicles and in some industrial processes. Carbon monoxide can be lethal when inhaled in an enclosed area. Heavy metals such as lead and mercury, which are highly toxic, also pollute the air.

Particulate matter from industries, motor vehicles, and heating units are other pollutants that can be hazardous to human health. If you spend a great portion of your time in a home with one or more smokers, you are likely to be exposed to and inhale larger amounts of particulates (as well as some toxic gases) from tobacco smoke than from other sources.[6]

Air pollution may affect only an immediate or local area, or present hazards to broad geographic regions. Increasingly, however, atmospheric scientists have learned about the global impact of some pollutants. Large-scale pollution problems—which once were studied separately—such as global warming and depletion of the protective ozone layer in the stratosphere—are now seen as interrelated dangers to the global environment.

URBAN AIR QUALITY

Air pollution affects most major cities worldwide, some worse than others, and urban air quality is a matter of concern to government leaders in most industrialized nations. In 1974, the World Health Organization and the United Nations Environment Programme set up a network to monitor air and water quality around the world and to establish guidelines for managing the earth's environment. The Global Environment Monitoring System (GEMS), as the network is called, collects data on the quality of urban air through a division called GEMS/Air. In late 1988, GEMS issued an assessment of urban air quality worldwide.

On a global scale, one of the major human-produced air pollutants is SO_2 from industries, power plants, and home heating, estimated to be about 176 million to 198 million tons (160–180 million tonnes [metric tons]) annually. "Over the past few decades, global emissions of SO_2 have risen by approximately 4 percent per year, a figure that corresponds to the increase in world energy consumption," noted the editors of the publication *Environment*, who analyzed and published excerpts from the GEMS report. Ninety percent of the SO_2 sources are in the Northern Hemisphere, although some nations—Norway, Sweden, and France among them—have reduced SO_2 emissions by one-half or more since the mid-1970s. Most industrialized nations have developed methods for controlling pollutants produced by burning fossil fuels. But putting controls into place can cost huge sums and may be a factor in whether or not air pollutants are reduced.

In developing countries, cities are growing rapidly, and urban growth includes expansion of industry and increased traffic, which brings higher demand for energy. These activities result in more air pollution. But as developing nations try to improve economic and social conditions, their urban and industrial growth takes precedence over pollution controls. Thus, not only do emissions of SO_2

increase worldwide, but other pollutants, such as NO_x, CO, and particulate matter, appear to increase each year as well.[7]

SOME CONTROLS ON POLLUTION

To control air pollution in the United States, Congress passed the nation's first Clean Air Act in 1963, which provided funds for state and local agencies to establish regulations for air quality. But the regulations were not adequate. By the end of the 1960s, it was clear that national standards were needed. The Clean Air Amendments of 1970 addressed that need. One part of the federal law set standards for emissions of various chemical compounds from mobile sources like cars and aircraft, and stationary sources such as industries and power plants.

The U.S. Environmental Protection Agency (EPA) has the authority to identify hazardous air pollutants and set standards for the amounts of these pollutants that may be emitted without endangering public health. Although the air in some cities has improved markedly since the 1970s, the nation has grown and industries and transportation have expanded, adding more and more pollutants to the atmosphere. Within the past few years, inventories of manufacturing plants and other businesses have revealed that several hundred different toxins are released into the atmosphere during any given year.

Today nearly two-thirds of the population live in what the EPA calls "non-attainment" areas. That means the air quality does not meet the EPA's standards for emissions of six pollutants: sulfur dioxide, carbon monoxide, nitrogen dioxide, particulates, ozone, and lead. Standards are based on careful research of the effects of these pollutants on health.

Air pollutants are known to cause respiratory diseases, cancer, and other serious illnesses. According to the American Lung Association, health problems from air pollution cost Americans $40 billion to $60 billion annually. Another study, conducted for the Association by the University of California at Davis, estimated that between 50,000 and 120,000 premature deaths each year could be linked to pollutants in the atmosphere.[8]

Air pollution not only threatens human health and life but also costs millions of dollars each year in damage to the environment. It is little wonder that controlling air pollutants is a major concern to citizens across the United States.

In poll after national poll, a vast majority of Americans say they want to see action in both the public and private sectors to clean up and protect the quality of the air they breathe. For example, a *Wall Street Journal*-NBC News poll showed that at least two-thirds of Americans surveyed said they were willing to pay up to $600 more for a car that would emit less pollution.

Surveys also have shown that an increasing percentage of the population supports tougher air pollution controls, which were put in place with the passage of amendments to the Clean Air Act of 1990. Some of the control measures, along with the problems they attempt to address, are discussed in the chapters ahead. This book also suggests ways in which all of us can do our part to improve air quality.

2
YELLOW SMOG, BROWN HAZE

"Some days I dread going into the city because of the air pollution," complained a teacher living outside a metropolitan area. "The powers-that-be say our air is clean, but that's not what my lungs say. Sometimes I can hardly breathe."

The teacher was not describing the air quality of Chicago, New York, Houston, or Los Angeles. Rather, she was concerned about the effects of dirty air in Indianapolis, an urban center in the heart of the nation's corn and soybean fields. Like most major cities across the United States and in other industrialized nations, Indianapolis has its bad days—times when the air seems thick with a yellow, brown, or gray haze, or smog.

THE CHEMICAL STEW

The term *smog* was coined about fifty years ago to refer to a combination of fog and air pollutants that frequently cast a shroud over Los Angeles, known as the city with the dirtiest air in the nation. At first officials thought the air pollutants came only from oil refineries in southern California. But by midcentury, air quality experts learned that smog was a combination of several pollutants.

Although the major component in smog is gaseous ozone, the gas itself is not a pollutant. Ozone is, in fact, essential for life on earth. For example, in the stratosphere—the layer of air far above the earth—ozone creates a gaseous shield that protects living things from ultraviolet rays of the sun. Without the protective layer of ozone, the well-being of every person on the planet is in jeopardy.

Smog ozone, on the other hand, forms in the troposphere—the layer of air closest to the earth—because of complex chemical reactions with substances that come from both anthropogenic (human-produced) and biogenic (naturally produced) sources. However, anthropogenic sources are responsible for most of the chemical compounds that lead to smog ozone.

The main anthropogenic source for emissions of both NO_x and VOCs is motor vehicles. Other sources include oil refineries and industries that use solvents such as paint, furniture, plastic, and computer-chip manufacturers. Metal-making companies, dry cleaning plants, gas stations, bakeries, and breweries also collectively produce large amounts of hydrocarbons.

Biogenic hydrocarbons come from trees and other vegetation. Some scientists believe these biogenic sources may play a more dominant role in ground-level ozone production than was previously thought. Recent studies at a rural Pennsylvania site and in the Atlanta, Georgia, urban area show that biogenic hydrocarbons are present during high levels of ozone. As an editorial report in the magazine *Science* explained, "60 percent of the Atlanta urban area is forested and about 400 tons of biogenic carbon are estimated to be produced each summer day. This is an amount comparable to the total of anthropogenic hydrocarbons emitted in the urban area. During the past decade the amount of anthropogenic hydrocarbons has been substantially reduced without a corresponding reduction in ozone."[9]

Another study, at MIT Energy Laboratory, also showed that ozone levels in rural areas can remain quite high because of VOCs emitted from vegetation. According to a report in *Technology Review*, researchers at the Energy Lab have developed a computer model that tracks the movement of known emissions of VOCs and shows how they mix and react. The model predicts ozone concentrations over the eastern part of North America. The magazine report notes: "The researchers have been surprised to find that even though cities spew out most of the precursor emissions humans produce, average ozone concentrations don't fall off abruptly in rural areas. . . . According to the model, the average levels of ozone are elevated both because the wind can carry ozone [over] long distances, and because the volatile organics emitted by vegetation can produce large quantities of the gas."[10]

The MIT researchers, along with other scientists, believe that because of the so-called background levels of ozone (biogenic emissions), emissions of human-produced hydrocarbons must be cut drastically, perhaps by more than one-half, in order to reduce smog in urban areas.

Usually, ozone linked to anthropogenic sources forms during warm, sunny days when the air is stagnant. Land forms play a part also. Los Angeles, for example, sits in a "basin," surrounded by mountains that tend to hold in smog for days or even weeks at a time, until winds move pollutants out.

The EPA has set a limit for smog ozone at 0.12 parts per million (0.12 ppm) parts of air over a period of an hour. Higher levels over a longer period are considered a danger to public health. Levels of some monitored air pollutants have dropped significantly since 1978, but ozone levels, which began to decline slightly nationwide, have been rising again. During an extremely hot summer in 1988, met-

A researcher adjusts a gauge on a smog chamber used to study the chemical reactions that take place when various air pollutants "stew" in the sun.

ropolitan areas such as Baltimore, Philadelphia, New York, Chicago, and Milwaukee experienced more than fourteen days of ozone pollution. Los Angeles recorded 148 days when ozone levels exceeded the federal limit. A total of ninety-four U.S. cities failed to meet federal air quality standards, some for the first time.[11]

EFFECTS OF SMOG OZONE

When smog ozone forms because of human activities, it adversely affects the health of millions of Americans. If people already suffer chronic illnesses such as asthma or heart disease, ozone can aggravate their problems. When there are high ozone levels, healthy individuals may experience lung dysfunction—coughing, "tightness" in the chest, or chest pain, for example—and such symptoms as burning eyes and a sore throat. Joggers, bicyclists, and people involved in strenuous outdoor activities are well advised to cut back on vigorous exercise during "smog alerts"—times when ozone concentrations are high.

Although high levels of ozone pollution can trigger a number of health problems, several studies have shown that long-term exposure to low levels of ozone may pose an even greater health risk. Smog ozone irritates membranes in the lungs and, over an extended period, causes permanent damage, reducing the ability of the lungs to resist respiratory diseases and heart problems. Some groups, such as the elderly, pregnant women, and infants, are more susceptible to ozone-related health risks than are others.[12]

Smog ozone also affects vegetation. Greenhouse experiments and field studies show that ozone is toxic to plants and destroys a variety of crops. An EPA study called the National Crop Loss Assessment Network (NCLAN) indicated that when ozone concentration during the growing season exceeds 0.04–0.05 ppm, there is a loss of 10 percent or more in the yield of such major cash crops as soybeans, peanuts, corn, and wheat. Reduced crop yields cost

American farmers between $2.5 billion and $3 billion each year, acording to EPA estimates.

Trees and shrubs often die or are stunted because of smog ozone. One laboratory study, published in *Science*, pointed out that ozone may "cause the greatest amount of damage to vegetation of any gaseous pollutant." According to the study, ozone reduced the rates of photosynthesis, the process by which plants capture and use solar energy. Evidence clearly showed that the reduced photosynthesis diminished tree growth and crop yields.[13]

A more recent study, conducted by the federal government and released in March 1990, found that most of the national parks in the United States are affected by air pollution. Trees are dying from damage due to smog ozone, and visibility in the parks has been reduced drastically because of pollutants, 90 percent of which come from nearby factories. Although the EPA has the authority to regulate emissions from industries, the agency has not enforced antipollution regulations, critics say. EPA regulators, on the other hand, claim they have been unable to track down the sources of foul air and smog over the nation's parks.[14]

Because of its reactive nature, smog ozone also can damage manufactured goods and natural building materials. For example, it causes rubber to crack, dyes to fade, and paint to erode. Ozone combined with acidic deposits is responsible for the corrosion of metal, concrete, and stone, particularly limestone, in various structures such as bridges, monuments, and statues.

OTHER SMOG INGREDIENTS

Another dangerous component in smog is carbon monoxide, a colorless, odorless gas. Carbon monoxide is produced by incomplete combustion. Motor vehicle exhausts are a primary source of carbon monoxide, although the gas also can be produced in faulty heating systems. Carbon monoxide is formed in cigarette smoke as well, and smokers may have high levels of the toxic gas in their bloodstreams.

Although carbon monoxide levels are dropping in most cities, physicians warn that urban residents with heart disease should limit their outdoor activities during times when carbon monoxide as well as ozone levels are high. What happens when carbon monoxide is inhaled? It binds with hemoglobin, a substance in red blood cells that carries oxygen. As a result of the binding, the amount of oxygen that reaches the heart, brain, and other vital organs is reduced. People exposed to small amounts of carbon monoxide over a long period of time may suffer from flulike symptoms, dizziness, or fatigue, or may appear to be drunk. Anyone exposed to high levels of carbon monoxide, as could occur in a closed garage when a motor vehicle is left running, could become disoriented, lose consciousness, or even die.

Microscopic particles of dust, soot, and chemical compounds called particulate matter are part of smog, too. In Los Angeles, daily smog reports for the four-county area—the South Coast Air Basin—include levels of particulate matter, called PM10. According to the *Los Angeles Times*, "PM10 stands for particles of 10 micrometers or less in diameter—about a tenth the diameter of a human hair . . . [and] only recently was equipment developed to forecast PM10 levels." The federal standard for a safe level of PM10 is "150 micrograms per cubic meter averaged over 24 hours . . . [which] translates to 100 on the pollutant standard index. Any reading over 100 exceeds the standard."[15]

CONTROLLING URBAN AIR POLLUTANTS

One of EPA's basic strategies for controlling urban air pollutants is to reduce human-produced hydrocarbon emissions and release of nitrogen oxides from stationary and mobile sources.[16] State agencies use this approach as well.

In southern California, for example, the South Coast Air Management District monitors emissions from such stationary sources as oil refineries and industries that use solvents or manufacture or use large amounts of paint.

Yet refineries and industries release only a small percentage of the total smog-producing emissions. At least 11 percent of these emissions in southern California come from small businesses such as gas stations and dry cleaning plants and from fumes from oil-based paints, varnishes, and stains used in homes and businesses. However, air quality experts say that motor vehicles are responsible for more than two-thirds of the region's NO_x and VOCs.

Nationwide, motor vehicles (and the fuel they burn) are a major source of pollutants that create smog in metropolitan areas. Over the years, a number of controls have been designed to curb smog-causing emissions from tailpipe exhausts and from fuel evaporation. For example, several states have passed laws that require gas station owners to install vapor recovery devices on pump nozzles. These prevent the escape of VOC fumes when gas is pumped into vehicle tanks. In some states, officials are demanding stricter enforcement of laws that require motorists to install pollution-control equipment or to repair faulty equipment on older cars.

During the past few years, auto manufacturers have added charcoal-canister devices to vehicles. These "on-board control systems," as they are called, capture gas vapors that otherwise would escape from the gas tank. The vapors pass through a carbon canister and are recycled into the engine, where they are burned, thus preventing the release of some hydrocarbons into the air.

The Clean Air Act of 1990 requires that on-board canisters installed on cars, trucks, and buses must capture vapors during refueling. As of 1994, new cars must be equipped with emission-control systems that reduce hydrocarbons by 35 percent and nitrogen oxides by 60 percent. Manufacturers also must issue warranties for emission-control systems, stating that the devices will function effectively for ten years or 100,000 miles (160,934.7 km).

NEW FUELS?

Rather than wait for new and tougher federal regulations to reduce emissions of hydrocarbons and nitrogen oxide emissions, California and several states in the Northeast, including New York and New Jersey, passed laws several years ago requiring changes in gasoline to reduce evaporation, a major source of pollutants that lead to smog.

The federal Clean Air Act requires that only reformulated gasoline be sold in cities with the highest levels of smog, such as Los Angeles. In reformulating gasoline, refineries reduce some aromatics, such as benzene, that help produce ozone and add MTBE (methyl tertiary butyl ether), which raises the oxygen levels of the gas, allowing it to burn cleaner.

Reformulated gasoline reduces pollution from older cars that use leaded gasoline and do not have emission-control devices. Lead gasolines are being phased out because lead is highly toxic to people who ingest it in fumes or other forms. But some cars on the road still use leaded fuel, as do motor bikes, road-building equipment, and other construction vehicles. Lead increases octane, or the ability of gas to resist engine knock; but other compounds, such as MTBE, accomplish the same results. The "new" gasoline is already being used in older cars driven in southern California, and refiners expect to produce a reformulated gas for newer cars.

To comply with stricter controls at state and local levels as well as those mandated by new amendments to the federal Clean Air Act, it is expected that car makers will produce an increasing number of vehicles that will run on so-called alternative fuels. Electric power or fuels such as natural gas, methanol, or ethanol are possible alternatives to gasoline. Each has some drawbacks, however.

Although electric cars produce no harmful emissions,

the energy has to be generated from sources that burn fossil fuels, indirectly causing pollutants to be released into the air. The amount of electricity that can be generated and stored in batteries for electric cars is limited, so batteries may need recharging frequently. Nevertheless, General Motors recently announced that it is developing an electric-powered car called the Impact model, which some designers say is the wave of the future.

To use natural gas as a fuel in vehicles, the gas is compressed into aluminum cylinders wrapped in fiberglass. The cylinders are installed under a vehicle or in the trunk and have proven to be safer and stronger than gasoline tanks. Engines that will burn compressed natural gas operate cleanly because the natural gas produces no particulates and only low levels of other pollutants.

Engines that burn natural gas have been installed in about 700,000 vehicles worldwide, including 30,000 in the United States. But at present, natural gas vehicles (NGVs) are not a practical option for private U.S. cars and trucks. The NGVs must be refueled often, and there are few stations that supply natural gas as a vehicle fuel. Also, the heavy fuel tanks increase the cost of manufacturing the vehicles. But NGVs work well as fleet vehicles—vans, trucks, and buses that travel within a particular area and return to a central location for refueling.[17]

In recent years, producers of methanol, which is processed from natural gas or coal, and ethanol, which is distilled from corn, have been touting their fuels as clean alternatives to gasoline. Both can be added to petroleum or used as pure alcohol fuels. As additives, they provide more oxygen to gasoline fuel, which means that the mixture burns more cleanly and cuts smog-producing emissions. However, methanol produces less energy than gasoline, so larger fuel tanks are needed to allow vehicles to travel as far on a tank of fuel as those burning gasoline. Burning methanol also produces formaldehyde, a gaseous compound that can cause leukemia and other blood diseases. (Methanol plus nearly all other VOCs are responsible for the formation of about 75 percent of all formaldehyde in the atmosphere, noted an EPA spokesperson in the Office of Air Quality.) In addition, formaldehyde triggers chemical reactions that produce smog.

Ethanol apparently does not pose as many health hazards as other fuels, but it costs more at the pump than gasoline. Both ethanol and methanol can corrode rubber or plastic engine parts. Although it is a relatively simple matter to produce alcohol-resistant parts for vehicles, auto manufacturers say that retooling factories for this purpose would be very expensive.

Another alternative fuel being developed is hydrogen, which primarily releases water vapor (steam). Researchers are now experimenting with a technology that extracts hydrogen from water, a process too expensive for use in the mass production of engines. But Daimler-Benz of West Germany has produced several models of a prototype car that runs on hydrogen, and the company engineers predict that hydrogen will be "the fuel of the future," according to a report in *Newsweek*. However, the hydrogen is highly flammable and must be carried in a heavy tank, holding only enough fuel for about 75 miles (120 km) of driving. It is expected to take more than a decade to develop a reasonably priced car able to run on hydrogen without frequent refills.[18]

CALLS FOR EXPANDED PUBLIC TRANSIT SYSTEMS

Another measure under discussion to control urban pollution is to reduce the number of cars on expressways by increasing mass transit facilities: bus, commuter train, and subway lines. Most transit systems are financed for the most part with federal and state tax funds; riders pay only a portion of the cost of operating public transportation systems. Thus, some taxpayer groups and government officials have objected to spending additional tax revenue for mass transit expansion, believing that transportation funds should be used instead to improve metropolitan expressways and streets.

In most cases, there has been much more public support for highway expansion and improvements than for mass transit. Powerful groups such as automobile clubs, trucking companies, and highway-building contractors long have pressured government officials to use gas taxes and other transportation funds for their special interests, namely, highway and road building and maintenance. Public transit riders seldom form organized groups and do not have the means to influence those responsible for funding transportation projects. As a result, highways frequently are built with little or no regard for broader transportation needs. Few funds are available to provide faster and more frequent public transportation services or conveniences such as parking facilities. Bus, commuter rail, and subway fares continue to increase to pay for services. Consequently, there is little that would lure people to use public transit systems.

Yet changes may take place, for a variety of reasons. For one, increased traffic has made many expressways in metropolitan areas more like stagnant parking lots, adding to commuters' frustrations and to air pollution problems. Some cities have proposed that motorists pay tolls to drive into city centers and that trucks be banned in downtown areas during peak traffic periods. As it becomes more difficult and costly to travel in and out of an urban center, an efficient transportation network, including both public and private means of travel—that is, affordable mass transit as well as roads, expressways, and highways—will be needed to move vehicles.

3
ACID RAIN

- All across the northeastern part of the United States and the mid-Atlantic states, in Canadian provinces, in Scandinavian countries and in other parts of Europe, thousands of lakes and streams have acid concentrations so high that aquatic food chains are destroyed, and fish die off.
- Vast numbers of red spruce, pine, fur, and other trees wither and die in North American and European forests, and tropical rain forests in Mexico and Central America are threatened.
- Metals are corroding, and world-famous structures such as the Taj Mahal, the Parthenon, the Statue of Liberty, and ancient Mayan ruins are being eaten away.
- Fresh paint on buildings and new cars fades quickly and may be marred with blotches of discoloration or indelible spots.

What has caused such damage and destruction? According to hundreds of scientific studies, acid rain is the culprit.

Over the past decade, scientists have published at least 3,000 papers on the causes and effects of acid rain.[19] Acidic pollution washing from the air also has been described in federal government reports, hundreds of popular magazines and newspapers worldwide, and on TV and radio news programs.

HOW ACID RAIN FORMS

The term *acid rain* is sometimes used very loosely to describe acidic substances in any type of precipitation—rain, snow, sleet, hail, dew, fog, or frost. But acid rain is only one part of acid deposition, which, technically, is the transfer from the atmosphere and deposit of both wet and dry substances on exposed surfaces. Dry acidic deposits may include dustfall or coarse particles that settle by gravitation, fine aerosols (such as smoke), and gases that are absorbed (taken in) or adsorbed (held on a surface).

Acidic substances form when gases—primarily sulfur and nitrogen oxides—are released into the air. Where do the gases come from? Originally, most nitrogen oxides were released when volcanoes erupted, when organic matter decomposed, or when forest fires burned. Some nitrogen oxides come from these and other biogenic sources such as lightning and sea salt spray. However, as is true in the formation of ground-level ozone, the precursors, or forerunners, of most acid-producing substances are anthropogenic. They come primarily from fossil fuel combustion.

An estimated 90 percent of global sulfur dioxide emissions are a result of fossil fuel burning. Other anthropogenic sources of sulfur dioxide emissions include smelting plants that melt or fuse copper, lead, and zinc ores; and producers of sulfuric acid.[20]

Once in the air, some acid-forming materials—large particulates—from power plants, industries, and mobile sources fall to the earth just a few miles away or within 18 to 30 miles (29-48 km). Other sulfur and nitrogen oxides rise high into the atmosphere, where winds carry the compounds hundreds to perhaps thousands of miles from their point of origin. During transport, the pollutants react with water vapor. Within hours to several days—or even weeks—later, this polluted water vapor may fall as acid precipitation.

Elevated chimneys, often called "tall stacks," on power plants and smelting facilities have been blamed for long-distance transport of sulfur compounds. It was once believed that effects from sulfur dioxide emissions could be abated by letting the pollutants disperse in air far away. So the tall stacks, some 1,300 feet (390 m) or more high, were built to rid local areas of pollution. But what goes up does come down—somewhere.

Most scientific studies show that prevailing winds, especially those from southwest to northeast, have carried acid rain precursors from coal-burning power plants in the Ohio River Valley to mountainous regions of the New England states and Canada. Canada has long claimed that at least 50 percent of the acid rain falling in its provinces is due to pollutants emitted in the United States. However, sulfur emissions also come from Canadian smelters and industries, and pollutants blow southward to form acid rain in the United States.

MEASURING ACIDITY

How is acidity of rain determined? Chemists use the pH (potential hydrogen) measurement to express the acidity of water solution in terms of hydrogen ion concentrations. (See the acid, or pH, scale on page 29.) Ions are electrically charged particles. Positively charged ions are called cations; anions are negatively charged ions. When cations and anions are equal in a solution, there is a balanced electrical charge, and the solution is considered neutral, shown as 7 on the pH scale.

Hydrogen ions are positively charged, and a solution

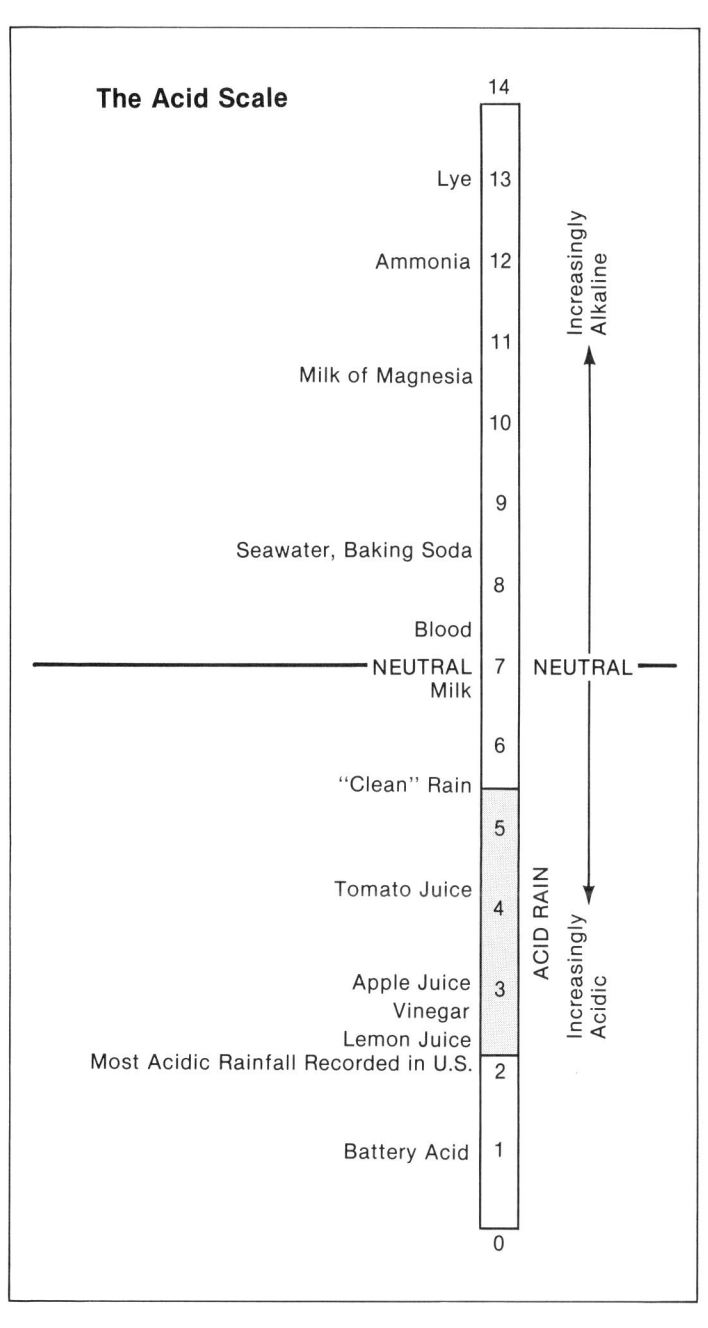

with more hydrogen ions than anions is acidic, expressed in a value below 7. If there are more anions than cations, a solution is alkaline, shown on the pH scale as a value above 7. Since the pH scale is logarithmic, each number represents a tenfold change in the concentration of hydrogen ions. A substance with a pH of 6 is ten times more acidic than distilled water, which is neutral (a value of 7). A pH 5 value indicates one hundred times more acidity; 4 is one thousand times and 3 is ten thousand times more acidic. In short, the lower the pH number, the more acidic the substance.

Acidity is not always harmful of course. Stomach fluids, which are essential for digestion, are highly acidic. Many foods and beverages are composed of organic acids. Apples and most carbonated soft drinks, for instance, have a pH of 3.0, and carrots register at a slightly acidic rate of 5.0. Some acidic substances help release nutrients from soils through a process that is essential for plant growth.

Theoretically, "normal" or "clean" rainfall (without pollutants) is considered slightly acidic due to carbon dioxide (CO_2) gas, which is a natural part of the atmosphere. Carbon dioxide dissolves in pure water to form a weak solution of carbonic acid having a pH of 5.6. Other acidic as well as alkaline substances occur naturally in the atmosphere and enter normal rainfall in small quantities. Thus, unpolluted rainfall still has a mix of ions that produces a pH of about 5.6. Precipitation with pH values substantially below 5.6 is considered acidic.

Rainfall in eastern North America and most of Scandinavia usually has a pH of 4 to 5, and some locations in western Pennsylvania and West Virginia have recorded pH levels between 3 and 4. In high elevations of the northeastern United States, the acidity in cloud covers can be similar to that of vinegar. The pH of fog in the Los Angeles area has dropped as low as 2, comparable to lemon juice.

ACID RAIN EFFECTS ON SOILS AND WATER

When acid rain falls, it usually does not have direct effects on lakes, streams, or plant life. Instead, once deposited on the ground, acid-producing substances travel through watersheds (the region drained by a river) to lakes, where many factors determine whether the water chemistry will be changed.

Some soils in the watershed may exchange nutrients, such as calcium and magnesium, for components of the acids; nutrients then may be leached (extracted) from the soil and enter water bodies while acids stay in the soil. In loose soils with alkaline materials, the acids can percolate through slowly and be modified so that less acid ends up in lakes and streams. Sulfuric acid, for example, can be held in some soils for a period of time. The watershed may contain materials such as calcium carbonate, the compound found in limestone, which can buffer or neutralize incoming acids, rather like the popular medications that neutralize excess stomach acids.

Along with soils, "virtually all lakes and streams have some acid-neutralizing capacities," said Orie Loucks, an ecologist from Miami University. Dr. Loucks, who has been studying acid rain effects for many years, pointed out that "if the surrounding watershed contains little neutralizing material, natural alkalinity levels in lakes and streams might be quite low, making these aquatic resources highly sensitive to even low levels of acidic inputs."

In North America, thousands of lakes and streams in the northeastern United States, portions of the northern Great Lakes states, and Canada have suffered damage from acidic deposition. In these areas, the water bodies are carved from hard rock, primarily granite. The soils are thin and have little buffering/neutralizing capacity. Surface waters are also vulnerable in southern Appalachia and

Florida and in the high elevations of such western states as Colorado, Washington, Oregon, and California.

Surface waters polluted by acids do not become acidic immediately. There may be enough chemical compounds in the watershed and bedrock to neutralize incoming acids for many years. However, when a lake or stream begins to lose its buffering capacity and the pH falls below 5, aquatic life begins to die off. Amphibians such as frogs and salamanders are very sensitive to low pH and may be the first species affected. Most shellfish die out in low pH waters, and a pH of 4.7 is lethal to most species of fish. At pH 4 only a few acid-resistant aquatic plants can survive. An acidified lake, which has no neutralizing capacity left, appears "clean"—clear blue—and is devoid of life.

In the early 1980s, Congress's Office of Technology Assessment conducted an inventory of surface waters in the twenty-seven-state area east of the Mississippi River. The agency found that well over half of the lakes and streams in the area—9,400 lakes and 60,000 miles (96,000 km) of streams—were sensitive to or had been altered by acidic inputs. Aquatic plant and animal life in approximately 3,000 lakes and 23,000 miles (36,800 km) of streams had been adversely affected by increased acidity of the surface waters.[21]

More recently, several eastern and mid-Atlantic states have completed studies of their own on the effects that acid inputs have on surface waters. Environmental departments in New York and Massachusetts, for instance, have found hundreds of lakes within their borders so acidic that most fish have died. If current levels of acid deposition continue, fish will be destroyed in half of Pennsylvania's streams by the year 2000.[22]

Even worse conditions exist across the Atlantic in Scandinavia. According to *The Earth Report*, "20,000 of Sweden's 90,000 lakes are acidified to one degree or another, and 4,000 of these are said to be totally devoid of fish life." In the southern half of Norway, "80 percent of the lakes and streams . . . are either technically 'dead' or on the critical list."[23]

Acid inputs also affect groundwater. Toxic forms of aluminum and mercury can be dissolved and released from soils by acidic waters and can percolate, or seep through, to water underground, a source of drinking water for nearly half of the U.S. population. Acid precipitation may wash such toxic substances as asbestos and lead from the atmosphere or leach them from soils, rocks, and even from water pipes.

Studies completed in the late 1980s show that mercury and other toxic substances also are washed from the air in acid rain and are deposited in lakes and streams, contaminating fish. Another effect of acid deposition is evident in some coastal waters. A 1988 study by the Environmental Defense Fund (EDF), an independent legal advocate group, found that nitrogen oxides in acid rain are contributing to excessive growth of algae along the eastern seaboard, especially in Maryland's Chesapeake Bay. Nitrogen is vital to plant growth, but an overload of nitrogen and other nutrients, such as phosphorus, leads to eutrophication—rapid growth of aquatic plants, especially algae. Algae use up the supply of dissolved oxygen in water, suffocating fish and other aquatic life. An overgrowth of algae also prevents needed sunlight from reaching marine plants and animals living at the bottom of the bay.[24]

DYING TREES

In the high-elevation forests of New York's Adirondack Mountains, Vermont's Green Mountains, and New Hampshire's White Mountains, more than half of the red spruce (conifers, or evergreen trees) have died over the past two decades. Growth of fir trees on North Carolina's Mount Mitchell and other Appalachian mountain peaks has been reduced. Pine growth has diminished in California's San Bernardino National Forest. Forests also are deteriorating in Canada and in European nations. "Creeping degradation," some have called it, but it is one more type of damage linked to acid deposition.

The first studies of acid rain effects on forests were done in West Germany during the early 1970s. Soil chemistry and forest growth were examined downwind of the Ruhr industrial region. West German researchers found that acid rain washes over several layers of leaves and branches before it reaches the ground. The foliage may be dusted with dry particles of acid-producing substances. Raindrops dissolve the particles and convert them to acids, which can wash through or linger on the leaves.

If acidic substances on the leaves and from precipitation reach the forest floor, the acid input can be two to four times more potent than acid rain alone. This can slow the breakdown of decaying matter that provides nitrogen and other plant nutrients. On the other hand, an overdose of nitrogen in acid deposits causes an imbalance in nutrients and creates stresses that lead to forest decline.

Long-term investigations of eight major forest areas in the United States have involved analysis of soil chemistry, leaf nutrition, and wood density. At each site, cores taken from trees show reduced growth. In one study of pines, researchers found that acidic deposits can plug needle pores, which help in the exchange of gases and in slowing water loss; damage to pores can hamper growth. In addition, acid rain causes the release of aluminum in soil, which destroys tree roots and blocks the intake of nutrients and water. Along with acidic deposits, smog ozone also creates stresses that weaken trees by destroying cell membranes in leaves and causing other damage.[25]

EFFECTS ON AGRICULTURAL CROPS

While there is little doubt that ozone causes extensive damage to agricultural crops, the same cannot be said for the effects of acid rain *alone*, except at low pH levels. Researchers at Oregon State University in Corvallis, Oregon, and at Argonne National Laboratory near Chicago used simulated acid rain (created in the laboratory) on crops in field chambers to determine how acidic solutions might affect such biological processes as nitrogen fixation and susceptibility to disease, insect injury, and cell damage.

At the Corvallis site, twenty-eight species of crops (including forage, grain, leaf, root, and tuber crops) were planted in pots containing the same type of soil. During the experimental period, which covered two growing seasons, the pots were placed inside vinyl, tentlike chambers in a huge field. For an hour and a half, three days per week over thirty weeks, technicians sprayed the plants with acidic solutions of pH 3.0, 3.5, 4.0, or a control rain of pH 5.6. Workers also regulated heat and air exchange, fertilization, pesticides, and irrigation. As a result of the experiments, researchers found that two-thirds of the crops were unaffected by acid rain. Of the remaining crops, half showed increases in yield, while the other half showed reduced yield.

In the Argonne experiment, soybeans were grown in field plots and in control chambers. The crops were exposed to acid rain and sulfur dioxide alone and in combination. "No harmful effects on soybean productivity occurred . . . in response to the acid rain stimulant," the study showed, although there was some injury to the leaves of soybeans exposed to acid rain inside control chambers, and decreased seed yield was the result of sulfur dioxide exposure.[26]

Other studies, conducted for the U.S. Department of Agriculture, indicate that crops such as clover, tomatoes, potatoes, cotton, alfalfa, and peanuts show little or no damage from acid rain. Farmers use fertilizers and lime on a regular basis to balance and improve soils. However, ozone combined with acid rain, as well as ozone alone, is damaging to some crops.

Patricia Irving, a research scientist, conducted a study several years ago at Argonne (Illinois) National Laboratory to determine the effect of acid rain on soybeans, a major U.S. crop. She also collected runoff water from experimental plots to determine how groundwater might be affected by acidic deposition.

THE POLITICS OF ACID RAIN CONTROLS

During the 1980s, members of Congress introduced a number of bills to amend the Clean Air Act, hoping to pass legislation for tighter controls on acid rain precursors. But the proposed laws created heated debate in Congress and solid resistance from the White House. The administration of President Ronald Reagan strongly opposed further regulations on power plants, automakers, and other industries responsible for sulfur dioxide and nitrogen oxide emissions, the acid rain precursors. That view also was reflected by some EPA administrators, appointed by Reagan, who seldom took aggressive action against polluters.

Leaders of public interest groups charged that the EPA's usual response was to call for more investigations into the problem. Critics also contended that representatives of industries as well as government officials in areas producing the greatest amount of acid rain precursors called for more studies as a way to stall passage of acid rain legislation.

Utilities in the Midwest and Southeast long resisted any new laws that would require expensive pollution controls and repeatedly fought antipollution laws in the courts. In spite of the vast amount of scientific data linking environmental damages to acid rain, utility companies claimed that acid rain was not a proven environmental problem. Utility representatives often quoted industry-funded studies, which concluded that soils or other environmental factors were the major contributors to acidification of lakes and streams and forest decline. Yet such statements did not necessarily reflect the emphasis of the studies and clearly were not the kinds of conclusions reached by the majority of scientists studying acid rain effects.

Industry representatives and some government officials also insisted that there was no direct cause-and-effect relationship between sulfur dioxide emissions and acidity in the environment. Those opposed to acid rain controls wanted proof that sulfur dioxide and nitrogen oxides form acidic substances in the atmosphere.

Since there is always uncertainty in scientific studies, particularly those dealing with many variables, scientists cannot make direct links between acid rain precursors and their effects. However, the evidence overwhelmingly links acid rain to ecological damage, and there is general scientific consensus (on a worldwide scale) that sulfur and nitrogen oxides are the main precursors of acid rain.

Acting on the scientific consensus, some Congressional lawmakers pressed for legislation that would curb acid emissions from Midwest power plants, which have accounted for much of the acid rain precursors that are transported to the northeastern United States and Canada. Finally, after ten years of Congressional and public debate, amendments to the Clean Air Act were passed in 1990, and the new law includes regulations to curb acid rain along with provisions to combat other air pollutants such as urban smog.

The Clean Air Act of 1990 requires that coal-fired power plants reduce sulfur dioxide emissions by about one-half, phasing in emission controls over several years. By the year 2000, sulfur dioxide emissions will be limited to 8.9 million tons (8 million tonnes) per year. Utilities can choose how they will clean up their operations.

Some companies may use conservation measures or cleaner low-sulfur coal to reach lower levels of emissions. The use of low-sulfur coal is expected to cause unemployment among Midwest miners. Most of the high-sulfur coal used in Midwest utilities comes from southern Ohio, Indiana, and Illinois mines and also from northern and southern Appalachia. However, the Clean Air Act calls for income assistance and training for coal miners who may lose their jobs because of the cleanup regulations.

Some power companies in the Midwest may continue burning high-sulfur coal, but the federal law requires that they use coal-cleaning technologies. These include crushing and washing coal to reduce sulfur content before burning and removing sulfur gases in the smokestacks or flues of coal-fired furnaces. One type of flue gas desulfurization system is known as "wet scrubbing." Jet streams of wet lime blast fumes in smokestacks, capturing from 70 to 95 percent of the sulfur dioxide before it gets into the atmosphere.

GLOBAL WARMING

While debates have raged over acid rain, arguments have been even more heated in regard to the greenhouse effect, or global warming. As with the acid rain controversy, on one side are scientists, environmentalists, and some government officials who want to control emissions from fossil fuel combustion and other gases that are linked to the greenhouse effect. On the other side are opponents of government intervention, who say there is no scientific certainty that the planet is getting warmer due to greenhouse gases. The anticontrol people believe more study is needed to determine whether the earth really is warming up.

THE GREENHOUSE THEORY

More than a century ago, scientists developed theories about climate changes that could be linked to minute changes in the composition of the atmosphere. A Swedish chemist, Svante Arrhenius, noted similarities between the earth's atmosphere and the glass enclosures of a greenhouse: both allow the sunlight to enter but prevent most of the solar heat from escaping. A glass or plastic greenhouse keeps plants warm by holding in heat and inhibiting air movement. The term *greenhouse effect* was coined to describe the warming of the earth.

However, the greenhouse effect on earth involves more than "holding in" heat. The earth's atmosphere is highly transparent to short-wavelength energy or sunlight. When visible light reflects from the earth's surface, energy is converted to a long-wavelength infrared radiation (see diagram on page 41). This radiation, or heat, is absorbed by opaque trace gases in the atmosphere, primarily water vapor and carbon dioxide, which are essential for life. Other trace gases, such as methane, nitrous oxide, ozone, and chlorofluorocarbons, also trap infrared radiation. Nitrogen and oxygen, which make up 99 percent of the atmosphere, do not absorb heat.

The gas molecules that do trap heat increase in temperature, and the heat then reradiates from the atmosphere in all directions, with some going back to the ground and some out into space. Without the greenhouse effect, too much heat would escape, and the earth would probably be too cold to sustain life. Yet an increase in carbon dioxide and other gases in the atmosphere may be creating too much heat for the earth. There is no evidence that the earth is heating so rapidly that it will burn up. But the buildup of greenhouse gases—the enhanced or accelerated greenhouse effect, usually referred to as simply the greenhouse effect—has prompted a great deal of scientific inquiry. Although the sources of greenhouse gases and their accumulation in the atmosphere are fairly well documented, there is scientific debate over the extent to which gases contribute to global warming.

WHY GREENHOUSE GASES HAVE INCREASED

The supply of carbon dioxide and other trace gases has been fairly stable on earth for millions of years, helping to maintain a delicate balance between the solar energy reaching

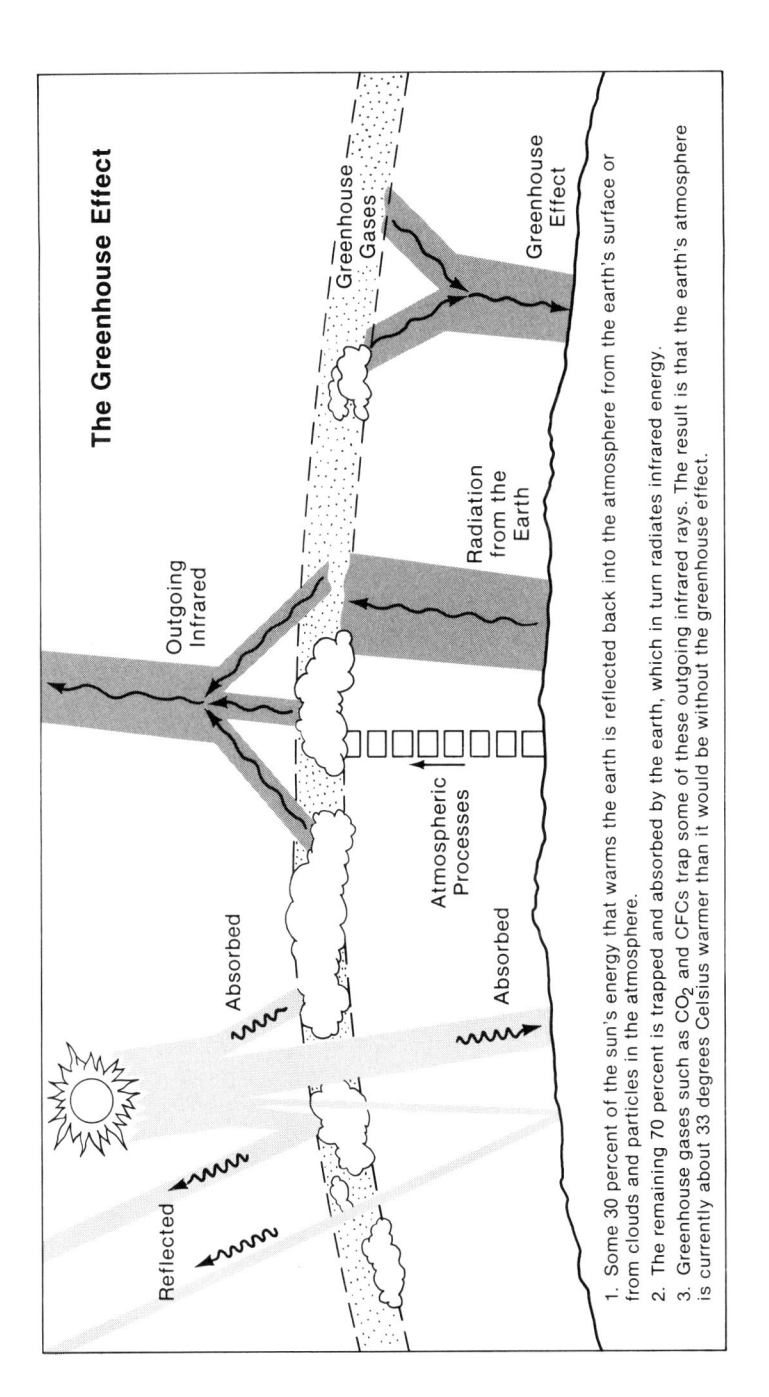

earth and the heat radiating out. In a process known as photosynthesis, plants capture sunlight and use solar energy to combine carbon dioxide and water, producing glucose, an important source of energy for animals and people. During photosynthesis, plants give off oxygen as a waste product; this is inhaled by animals and people, who in turn exhale carbon dioxide produced when food is oxidized, or used by their bodies. Thus, living plants and animals are one source of carbon dioxide released into the atmosphere. Other natural pools, or reservoirs, of carbon dioxide include the oceans and fossilized forms of carbon such as oil, gas, and coal.

But human activities, particularly fossil fuel combustion since the industrial revolution, have been responsible for increasing amounts of carbon dioxide, the major greenhouse gas (along with water vapor) in the atmosphere. In recent years, vast amounts of the earth's forests, particularly in the Southern Hemisphere, have been cut or burned to make way for farming and raising dairy and meat animals. In the tropical rain forests, 50 acres (20 hectares) are being cleared away per minute. "The world's forests are being destroyed at a rate of one football field-sized area every second," wrote Senator Albert Gore, Jr., of Tennessee, who has long been concerned about environmental issues.[27]

Because trees are "sinks," or holding places, for carbon dioxide, the destruction of forests has released billions of tons of carbon dioxide into the atmosphere. Cutting and burning forests, along with the increasing use of fossil fuels due to population and economic growth, have increased global carbon emissions each year since the end of World War II. "It took 10 years for [emissions] to go from two billion to three billion tons, but just six more years to get up to four billion," wrote Christopher Flavin of Worldwatch Institute.[28]

Since 1957, scientists have monitored the carbon dioxide levels in the atmosphere at a station atop a volcanic mountain in Hawaii. The location was selected because it is isolated from industrial pollutants and biogenic sources of carbon dioxide that might affect readings. Measurements show a steady increase in carbon dioxide over three decades. The graph on page 44 shows how a number of nations contribute to global warming via deforestation and energy consumption.

More recently, teams of researchers from the Soviet Union, Europe, and the United States have been testing Antarctic and Greenland ice cores that have built up over hundreds of thousands of years, trapping air bubbles. The ice core samples show that 160,000 years ago, during a glacial period (or ice age), the carbon dioxide level was 180 ppm. Carbon dioxide concentrations increased to about 270 to 280 ppm with a corresponding rise in temperature during interglacial (or warming) periods. Atmospheric scientists have determined that carbon dioxide has increased by 25 percent over the past century, from about 280 ppm to about 350 ppm today, a much more rapid and larger increase than any other known in human history.[29]

Human activities are responsible for increases in other greenhouse gases, such as nitrous oxide that comes from fertilizers and motor vehicle exhausts and chlorofluorocarbons (CFCs or Freons) that come from such sources as foam plastics, air-conditioning units, and gas-propelled spray cans. Although substitutes for CFCs are now being used in the United States, CFCs are still components of many existing products; when released, the gases become harmful pollutants.

Methane is another gas that adds to the warming "blanket" swaddling the earth. It comes not only from burning natural gas but also from such sources as the digestive tracts of cattle and other domestic animals, from rice paddies, and from termite nests that vent the gas into the air. Studies conducted in the United States and Europe during the past decade show that the amount of methane in the atmosphere has doubled over the past 200 years. It is not

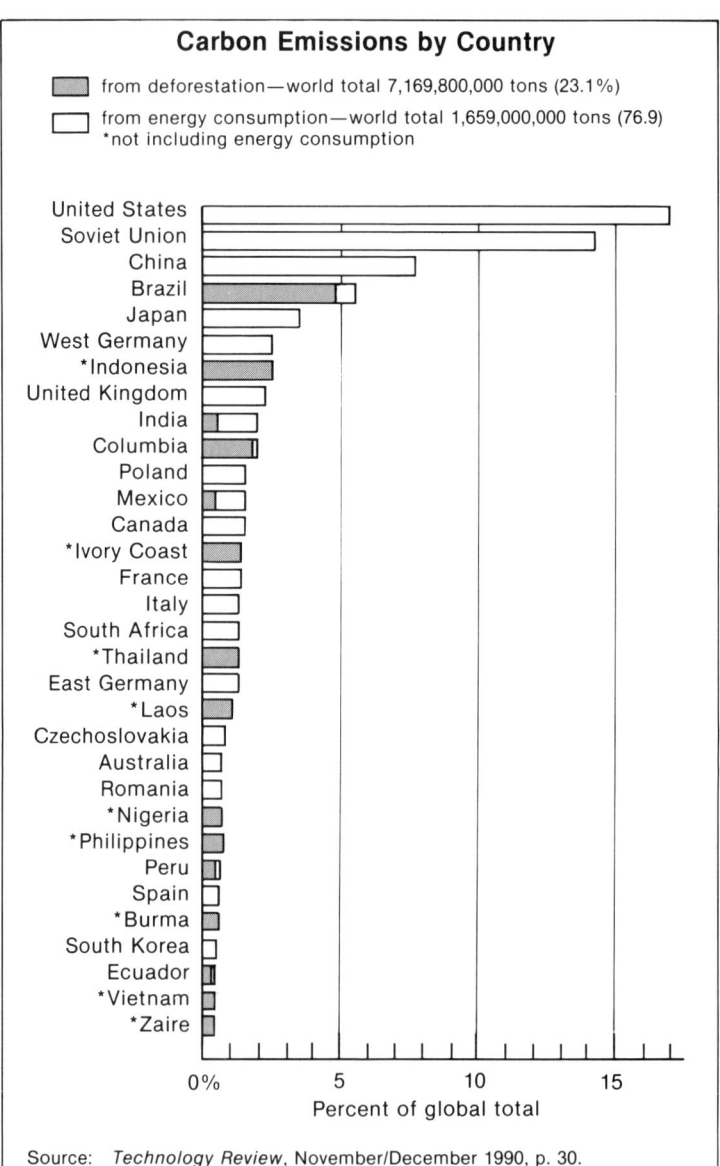

certain why methane has increased. But researchers have found that termite populations explode in areas where forests have been cleared for agriculture. Cattle production and acreage planted in rice also have grown worldwide. Scientists have not determined how much these sources contribute to the accelerating greenhouse effect, but they believe that trace gases like methane accelerate climate changes brought on by increases in carbon dioxide.[30]

HOW WARM, HOW SOON?

With the steady buildup of greenhouse gases, the average worldwide temperature has risen about 1 degree Fahrenheit (or about $\frac{1}{2}$ degree Celsius) over the past 100 years. A temperature rise of 1 degree or less seems too small to worry about. But consider this: During the last ice age, which ended about 10,000 years ago, the average global temperature was only about 8 or 9 degrees colder than it is now, and the average temperature rose only a few degrees every *thousand* years or so. If greenhouse gases continue to accumulate at the present rate, scientists predict that the average global temperature, now at 59 degrees Fahrenheit (15°C), will increase dramatically in a relatively short time (see graph on page 46).

A well-known climatologist, James Hansen, has forecast a warming of up to 9 degrees Fahrenheit by the year 2030 or 2040 if current emissions of greenhouse gases continue to rise. Hansen, who is director of the National Aeronautics and Space Administration's Goddard Institute of Space Studies, also testified in 1988 before a Congressional Committee that he is "99 percent certain" that the warming trend brought on by greenhouse gases already has begun. In spite of criticism from other scientists, who say that such certainty is premature, Hansen continues to stand by his views. At the same time, he and many other scientists point out that no one has absolute proof about global warming and its causes and effects.[31]

Since scientists cannot create the many variables of

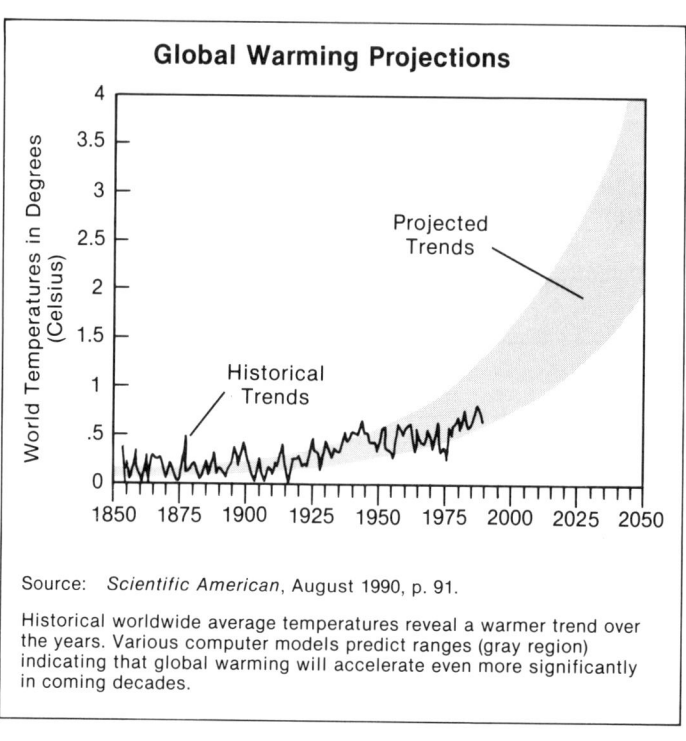

Source: *Scientific American*, August 1990, p. 91.

Historical worldwide average temperatures reveal a warmer trend over the years. Various computer models predict ranges (gray region) indicating that global warming will accelerate even more significantly in coming decades.

the Earth's weather in a laboratory, they use mathematical equations "to represent the basic physical laws that govern the motions of the atmosphere, oceans, and ice," as Stephen Schneider, head of an international research group at Boulder, Colorado, explained in a *World Monitor* article. The equations are run on a supercomputer that takes into account such weather variables as winds, sunlight, and precipitation for a specific area of the earth. Schneider pointed out that computer models in various parts of the world agree on a steady rise in average global temperature with increases in greenhouse gases, but the models "disagree markedly as to the specific regional distribution of climatic changes" and when they will occur.[32]

There are also uncertainties about whether global warming will produce more clouds, which could help cool the earth because they reflect the sun's rays. But clouds also can trap heat that rises from below. Since cloud formations vary greatly and are scattered over broad areas, there is no clear picture of their role in climate change. And cloud formations have not been included in the computer calculations of how weather variables may affect global warming.

Another major problem in computing global warming calculations is getting accurate temperature measurements over the surface of the earth. A report in *Science News* explained that the surface measurements may not represent true global temperatures because "The [measuring] network does not sufficiently cover vast regions of the remote oceans, and urban heat from developing cities may artificially boost temperatures at land stations."[33]

Satellite instruments that scanned and recorded temperatures of the earth's lower atmosphere from 1979 to 1988 show "large fluctuations" in global temperatures "but no obvious trend for the 10-year period," according to NASA scientists. Yet the scientists noted that the data they analyzed do not necessarily disprove or prove the global warming theory because the time period for the temperature record is too brief to determine whether global warming has actually begun.[34]

Whatever the uncertainties about possible global warming, recent articles in scientific journals and reports in major U.S. newspapers indicate broad scientific agreement that the buildup of greenhouse gases can contribute to climate changes. In late 1990, about 500 scientists from around the globe met in Geneva, Switzerland, to discuss global warming and predicted that if the emissions of greenhouse gases are not curbed, global temperatures could increase perhaps 5.4 degrees by the end of the twenty-first century.

EFFECTS OF GLOBAL WARMING

Computer calculations suggest that rising temperatures will result in shifting precipitation patterns and expansion of frost-free regions of the world. Most climatic models indicate that there would be reduced rainfall and snow across the latitudes that include the United States. In other words, there would be more droughts. At higher latitudes—in Canada, for example—precipitation likely will increase, and the growing season will be longer. Increased rainfall also is expected in the lower latitudes, south of the United States.

Alterations in precipitation patterns can affect water supply and distribution, changing where crops are grown and animals are raised. If the grain belt in the middle of the United States becomes hotter and drier, corn crops would have to be grown farther north, perhaps in Canada. Weeds and pests would change with altered climate. Some forestlands would be reduced.

Another expected impact of global warming is a rise in sea level brought on by ice and snow melts that run off into the oceans. Scientists also believe that oceans could expand thermally; warming could reduce the water density and increase volume. Warmer oceans would bring about more severe hurricanes and other violent storms. Higher sea levels would erode or inundate shorelines, destroying homes, businesses, roads, and ports worldwide. Rising sea levels also would force salt water into rivers, streams, and groundwater sources, reducing drinking water supplies and altering entire ecosystems. Intrusion of salt water into freshwater systems, along with flooding, would adversely affect agricultural production.

WHERE'S THE "WHITE HOUSE EFFECT"?

During his election campaign, President George Bush declared that he would use the "White House effect" in efforts to combat an enhanced greenhouse effect. However, several members of Congress and representatives of environmental groups believe that the president and some of his staff have been "dragging their feet" on the issue. The Bush administration has emphasized the scientific uncertainty in regard to the greenhouse effect, expressing doubts about whether climate change will actually take place.

Yet more than 700 members of the National Academy of Sciences (about half of the membership) and 49 Nobel Prize winners in the United States called global warming "the most serious environmental threat" of our time. In a letter to President Bush, the scientists warned that the buildup of greenhouse gases brought on by human activities could produce dramatic changes in climate.

Critics say that Bush has followed the approach taken by his chief of staff, John Sununu, who has appeared more concerned about the political and economic costs of air pollution controls than about protecting public health and the environment. Sununu's comments on a TV talk show reflected his views: "There's a little tendency by some of the faceless bureaucrats on the environmental side [of the administration] to try and create a policy in this country that cuts off our use of coal, oil, and natural gas. I don't think America wants not to be able to use their automobiles," Sununu said.

Serious arguments for curbs on fossil fuel use have *not* included the idea of banning motor vehicles altogether but instead have advocated widespread energy conservation, including use of alternative fuels and less gas guzzling in automobiles. "If vehicles averaged 50 miles [80 km] to the gallon rather than the current 20 [32 km], automobile carbon emissions would fall to 273,000,000 tons [246 million tonnes], half of what they are today," a report in *USA Today* noted.[35]

Some government officials justify their lack of action on fossil fuel curbs by citing several studies that in effect conclude that global warming is some kind of myth. But the studies had not been subjected to review by other scientists, a standard procedure for serious scientific research. One research report prepared for the George C. Marshall Institute predicts that a cooling trend over the next century will offset any greenhouse warming. But as a *Science* article pointed out, noted atmospheric scientists have labeled the report more of a political document than a scientific one. Only a few scientists, most of whom have not specialized in greenhouse research, are skeptical about global warming.[36]

Apparently taking its cue from the White House, those against tougher controls on greenhouse gases have used the Marshall report to downplay global warming. *Forbes* magazine, aimed at business people and industrialists, published a lead article in December 1989 titled "The Global Warming Panic," which asserted that the public and most of the press are getting hysterical over an accelerating greenhouse effect. That same month a columnist in *Car and Driver* related global warming to a kind of paranoia, writing that he was "pretty sure that laughing is the right response to the whole global-warming scare" and that "global warming is just one more rewrite of the old Chicken Little fable [that the sky is falling]."[37]

A point that the skeptics in the global warming debate ignore is that cutting back on fossil fuel use would help curb many air pollutants. Donella H. Meadows, adjunct professor of environmental studies at Dartmouth College, put it this way in a *Los Angeles Times* editorial:

> *The primary action necessary to combat a greenhouse effect is to use fossil fuels much more efficiently. Whether there is a greenhouse effect or not, energy efficiency would improve the environment, the balance of payments and the general economy. But it would greatly inconveni-*

ence the oil, coal, electricity and automobile industries, among others. Hence the eagerness in some political camps not to believe in the greenhouse effect, and to cite only the side of the argument that feeds such bias.[38]

COOLING IT

The United States and six other industrialized nations—Canada, England, France, Italy, Germany, and Japan—produce about 40 percent of the carbon dioxide spewed into the atmosphere each year from fossil fuel combustion. Although leaders of these nations agreed during an economic summit that greenhouse gases could threaten the environment and could bring about climate changes with drastic economic consequences, no national leader yet has presented a specific strategy for cooling the earth. Some governments, however, are preparing for possible *effects* of a global warming. According to a feature in *The New York Times:*

Already, state and local governments along the coast of the United States are starting to plan for a possible long-term rise in the sea level, and a few have taken action to cope with it.

Agricultural researchers are stepping up efforts to develop heat-resistant and drought-resistant crops....

The electric power industry in America is planning how to meet the increase in the demand for power for air-conditioning that would surely result from global warming.[39]

Although many researchers and environmental groups believe that it is necessary to plan and initiate ways to adapt to climate change, they also stress reduction of fossil fuel use as one of the most important steps in dealing with global warming.

"Many energy planners favor increased reliance on nuclear power, which today generates about 17 percent of the world's electricity, since its use does not emit carbon dioxide or the pollutants that cause acid rain," write John Gibbons and his coauthors in a special issue of *Scientific American* that focuses on managing the earth. (Gibbons is director of the Office of Technology Assessment, which advises the U.S. Congress on technology-related issues.) The authors point out, however, that accidents at nuclear plants and concerns about safe disposal of highly radioactive nuclear waste "have tarnished public reception of reactor safety and reliability." As a result, since 1978 no new construction of nuclear plants has been initiated. But other energy sources, such as solar power, waste-to-energy plants (burning garbage to produce energy), and production of geothermal energy (tapping underground steam that comes from hot springs and geysers) are being expanded.

More important, the authors describe many ways to decrease oil consumption and improve energy efficiency. But they note that "even dramatic improvements in energy efficiency will not be sufficient to protect the environment if they are confined to the industrialized world."[40]

Developing countries of the world need inexpensive fossil fuels to improve their living conditions. China, for example, plans to expand its industries and burn vast amounts of coal, the only feasible energy resource at this time. But increases in coal burning will not only add to the carbon dioxide overload but also will increase sulfur dioxide in the atmosphere. Other nations will continue to clear forests, destroying more carbon dioxide sinks, as they attempt to provide more food and other products for growing populations.

Still, energy experts in the United States continue to urge energy conservation as one of the basic actions individuals can take to help reduce carbon dioxide emissions and other gases that contribute to climate change. Since the 1970s, when there was an oil shortage, Americans have greatly improved energy efficiency—by about 40 percent, according to the Union of Concerned Scientists (UCS). But the organization believes much more can and must be done, pointing to the fact that major industrialized countries like Japan and Germany have achieved a high standard of living but use only half as much energy per person as Americans do.

5
ATTACK ON THE OZONE LAYER

Chlorofluorocarbons (CFCs) make up at least one-sixth of the human-produced gases responsible for global warming. But CFCs are playing another treacherous role in the atmosphere. The compounds stick around for up to 150 years, slowly working their way up to the stratosphere some 15 miles (about 25 km) above the earth's surface, where they release chlorine that attacks ozone molecules.

Unlike the ozone pollutant formed at ground level, ozone in the stratosphere is essential for life. As explained earlier, ozone absorbs the sun's ultraviolet radiation that otherwise could harm crops, marine life, and human health.

WHAT HAPPENS IN THE STRATOSPHERE?

In the stratosphere, solar radiation breaks down molecular oxygen (O_2) into two oxygen atoms (O), which in turn combine with additional O_2 to form ozone (O_3). Some of the ozone is reconverted to oxygen, and the photochemical process continues, creating a very thin layer of ozone that surrounds the earth. The gaseous ozone not only absorbs UV radiation but also determines stratospheric temperature and thus plays a role in the circulation patterns of the stratosphere.

Although ozone is constantly produced by the photochemical process, it is also destroyed by chemical reactions involving such gases as nitrogen, hydrogen, and chlorine. In addition, the amounts of ozone change with the seasons as winds transport ozone throughout the stratosphere. But, over centuries, the production and loss processes have balanced, keeping just the right amount of ozone around the planet to protect all life from too much UV radiation. However, that delicate balance now is threatened.

During the past decade, atmospheric studies at the North and South Poles have shown that chlorine monoxide from human-produced CFCs and compounds called halons (gases used in fire extinguishers) accumulate in the stratosphere. Reactive chlorine then comes into contact with clouds of microscopic ice particles formed from water vapor and chemical compounds. These polar stratospheric clouds (PSCs), as they are called, provide a surface for chemical reactions to take place. Basically, chlorine nitrate and hydrogen chloride, which are relatively inert, are converted to active chlorine compounds that attack and destroy ozone. Each free chlorine atom can destroy 100,000 molecules of ozone before its chain reaction has been completed.

Because of their long lifetimes, CFCs and halons are expected to increase in the stratosphere even if emissions of these compounds remain the same or drop in the next few decades. In other words, the compounds that have been accumulating are moving slowly from the troposphere into the stratosphere.

CFC RESEARCH

When CFCs were first developed in the early 1930s, they seemed to be almost perfect chemicals. Since CFCs are nonflammable, nontoxic, and noncorrodible, they can be used in a variety of products without the worry of drastic changes in their properties or the threat of fire and other hazards. But the great stability of CFCs also allows them to survive for many years and "pile up" in the troposphere, eventually moving into the stratosphere, where they can destroy ozone.

In 1974, two researchers from the chemistry department of the University of California at Irvine, F. Sherwood Rowland and Mario J. Molina, released a study proposing that CFCs percolated through the troposphere into the stratosphere, altering the chemistry of the protective ozone layer. That proposal was hotly debated, but atmospheric scientists in many nations followed up with studies that confirmed the findings of Rowland and Molina.

At the same time, the possible threat to the ozone layer caught the attention of the general public, and people called for bans on CFCs in aerosol sprays. In 1978, the U.S. Congress passed legislation that outlawed the manufacture of CFC aerosols. Canadian, Swiss, and Scandinavian governments took similar actions. However, CFCs still are used widely in aerosol products manufactured in other nations and in a variety of U.S. products, including refrigerators, air conditioners, foam packaging, and solvents for cleaning computer circuit boards.

In 1985, public attention again focused on the damaging effects of CFCs. British atmospheric scientists, who operated an observation station at Halley Bay on the coast of Antarctica, published a startling report: Concentrations of ozone over Antarctica had been dropping during September and October, the austral (Southern Hemisphere) spring. During this season, and only then, there appeared to be a thinning of the protective ozone layer.

The scientists, who were with the British Antarctic Survey team, had been collecting data for decades. They found that almost half of the ozone over the South Pole disappeared or failed to appear every season. The phenomenon, which later was dubbed a "hole," occurred repeatedly, with increasing amounts of ozone loss each season between 1977 and 1984. At another British station, on the Argentine Islands, about 1,000 miles (1,600 km) to the northwest, similar ozone losses had been recorded.

After the British discovery of the ozone hole, U.S. researchers reviewed data from land-based instruments that have been used at various sites since the 1950s to measure ozone distribution on a global scale. Atmospheric scientists also reviewed ozone data from satellites. They found that satellite instruments had recorded seasonal drops in ozone over Antarctica, but the computer program used to read the data had been designed to reject major decreases or increases in ozone levels as "improbable." Using a revised program, American researchers concluded that their data supported the British findings. The ozone hole was very real.

EXPEDITIONS AND OBSERVATIONS

In spite of computer and satellite data, the ozone-science community knew that much more information was needed. Leading U.S. atmospheric scientists and engineers formed an interagency team to step up ozone research. The researchers have taken part in several expeditions to McMurdo Station, a National Science Foundation (NSF) site in Antarctica. At the station, researchers launched high-altitude balloons with electrochemical sensors to measure ozone. The balloons travel into the stratosphere and beam findings from sensors back to instruments being read by specialists at the observation station.

One of the other instruments used at McMurdo was a visible light spectrometer that measures visible wavelengths, or series of color bands, from light sources—the sun and moon. Since various chemicals in the stratosphere absorb different wavelengths or colors, the instrument could measure the amount of such compounds as chlorine dioxide and nitrogen dioxide in the thinning ozone layer of Antarctica. Data showed that there were exceedingly low levels of nitrogen dioxide, which inhibits ozone loss when it "ties up" active chlorine. At the same time, there were elevated amounts of chlorine dioxide, a by-product of the chemical reaction that takes place in polar clouds, and chlorine monoxide, which actually destroys ozone.

To carry out additional research, National Aeronautics and Space Administration (NASA) planes flew over Antarctica to collect air samples. One of the aircraft was a DC-8, a former passenger plane set up like a laboratory, and the other was a modified spy plane called an ER-2. Although the DC-8 usually flew below the stratosphere, scientists on board used laser radar instruments to monitor the Antarctic ozone hole. The ER-2 was able to fly at altitudes ranging from 7.5 to 11 miles (12–18 km) above the earth's surface, well into the stratosphere where ozone is being depleted. Instruments on the ER-2 measured distributions of ozone, chlorine and nitrogen compounds, and the makeup of ice crystals in the stratosphere.

In late 1990, NASA reported that satellite data showed that the Antarctic ozone hole was even larger than it had been in 1987 and 1989, the two worst years for ozone depletion. Although the exact amount of ozone depletion has not been fully calculated to data, NASA also noted that ozone levels throughout the Southern Hemisphere were as low as for any previous years.

RESEARCH OVER THE NORTH POLE

As research was conducted in Antarctica, Norwegian scientists noted an ozone deficit over the Arctic in mid-1986. But the thinning appeared minor and was only transitory. Then, in 1988, a team of American atmospheric scientists went to Thule, Greenland, to study the chemistry of the stratosphere over the North Pole. An airborne expedition similar to the Antarctic flights was conducted in 1989. The

A scientist aboard a DC-8 flying laboratory operates the electronic data handling system that measures ozone and polar stratospheric clouds.

findings: Large amounts of chlorine dioxide were detected over the Arctic, and climatic conditions were similar to those of the Antarctic—swirling winds, cold temperatures, and stratospheric clouds that contribute to the ozone-destroying process.

The researchers also found low levels of nitrogen dioxide compared to the "standard" chemistry of the atmosphere in which there is enough NO_2 to convert active chlorine compounds into nonreactive forms. Thus, all the factors put together strongly suggested that the same phenomenon occurring in Antarctica is also happening in the Arctic.

However, researchers have concluded that the ozone losses over the Arctic are far less than those over the Antarctic. A report in *Science* noted: "In the Antarctic, as much as half of all the stratosphere's ozone has been destroyed in some years, with the losses reaching more than 95% at some altitudes. Over the Arctic, total ozone destruction probably did not exceed a few percent and the hardest hit layers, those at just above 20 kilometers [12 miles], might have lost only 15 to 20% of their ozone."[41]

EFFECTS OF OZONE DEPLETION

Since ozone losses have been observed over the poles, what has been happening to the ozone layer on a worldwide scale? A panel of scientists reported that global stratospheric ozone has decreased about 2.5 percent, on average, from the mid-1970s to the mid-1980s. The greatest ozone losses have been in the tropics, although ozone losses also have been recorded over the United States, Europe, China, Japan, and part of the Soviet Union.

If stratospheric ozone continues to diminish worldwide, increased radiation could occur over highly populated areas in the midlatitudes, which could lead to a variety of human health problems. Health hazards include damage to the immune system, which would weaken the body's ability to fight diseases, and higher incidences of such eye disorders as cataracts, retinal damage, and corneal tumors.

Increased UV radiation also would bring about more cases of skin problems such as premature aging of the skin and higher incidences of squamous-cell carcinoma, a type of nonmalignant cancer that affects mostly light-skinned people. Dark-skinned people are relatively safe from nonmalignant skin cancer because the melanin pigment in the skin provides protection from UV damage.

Currently, more than 500,000 Americans each year develop skin cancer. With each 1 percent loss in ozone, the skin cancer rate is expected to increase by 3 to 6 percent. Although the vast majority of skin cancers can be cured, one type, melanoma, is more dangerous and affects people of all skin colors. According to the American Cancer Society, 1 of every 128 Americans will develop malignant melanoma during his or her lifetime, compared to 1 in 1,500 Americans who developed the disease during the 1930s. Medical experts urge people to take protective measures to prevent nonmalignant skin cancer, such as wearing wide-brimmed hats and clothing that covers the skin when exposed to the sun for long periods, limiting "sunbathing," and using lotions or sunblocks that can screen out harmful UV rays.

How does UV radiation affect land-based plants and marine life? According to laboratory studies, enhanced UV radiation could slow the process of photosynthesis, reduce leaf area, and decrease water use efficiency in many plants.[42] Thus, yields of some crops such as soybeans would decrease, costing billions of dollars in crop losses.

Aquatic life also could be endangered by ozone depletion. Although some aquatic species, such as anchovy larvae, have developed a tolerance for increased UV radiation, greater ozone depletion might result in abnormal development of larvae or kill off larvae, which are used worldwide in animal feeds. There is some speculation that organisms such as blue-green algae that are unharmed by UV light could dominate aquatic systems.

Indirectly, added UV radiation is expected to stimulate climatic conditions that promote smog—ozone pollution. Studies show that "ozone concentrations would peak earlier in the day and at greater distances from the source, with the result that a larger human population would be exposed and at risk."[43]

RESISTANCE TO CONTROLS

In spite of the many studies confirming the hazards posed by CFCs, there was much resistance to sanctioning controls on their use. For example, representatives of the Du Pont company, the world's largest manufacturer of CFCs, had long insisted that the gases were no real danger to the ozone layer and that such assertions were based on faulty science. As has been the case with controls on other air pollutants, industries and government officials opposed to regulations first called for "clear scientific evidence" that there is a serious threat to the ozone layer.

By the mid-1980s, however, new scientific findings had made it clear that it was no longer a matter of whether atmospheric pollutants should be controlled but when those controls should be put into effect.

But decisions on control regulations did not come quickly. CFC manufacturers argued that a freeze or cutback in U.S. production of CFCs would result in job losses and in the end would make little difference without worldwide restrictions on CFCs. Many other nations not only make wide use of CFCs but some have increased production of these chemicals for a variety of purposes. Japan and Western European countries, including Britain, West Germany, and France, join the United States as major producers and consumers of CFCs. In addition, developing countries and the Soviet Union have been increasing their CFC use over the past decade. Naturally, U.S. manufacturers did not want to be singled out for cutbacks while industries in other parts of the world continued to enjoy profits from products that contain CFCs.

For many years, directors of the United Nations Environment Programme (UNEP) had called for worldwide restrictions on CFC use and were finally able to set up a Convention for the Protection of the Ozone Layer. In March 1985, representatives of twenty-eight nations, including the Soviet Union, signed an agreement that established a framework for cooperative research on ozone depletion. The next step would be convincing the participating nations to sign a protocol, or a draft for a treaty, that would regulate the use of CFCs and halons on a global scale.

The U.S. government proposed a freeze on production of CFCs and halons with phaseouts in several stages over ten to fourteen years. However, industry and trade specialists argued that developing effective substitutes for CFCs and halons would take time, which might allow manufacturers in other nations to gain a competitive edge. European nations, Japan, and the Soviet Union opposed cuts in halons used for military and other purposes, and Japan did not want reductions in CFCs imposed on its fast-growing electronic industries.

In spite of the opposition, representatives from the United States, the European Community (a bloc of Western European nations that cooperate on economic matters), Japan, and other nations met in Montreal, Canada, in September 1987 to sign an international treaty called the Montreal Protocol. According to the treaty, the industrialized nations—major consumers of CFCs and halons—agreed to cut the use of these chemicals in half by 1998. In a later amendment, the signatory nations agreed to a complete phaseout of CFCs by the year 2000. The treaty also requires signatory nations to ban imports of bulk CFCs and products containing CFCs that come from nonsignatory countries.

Regulations for the use of CFCs in developing countries are less stringent because most of them are just beginning to establish industries that manufacture CFC products. At a May 1990 conference in Geneva, Switzerland, the UN proposed that member nations of UNEP assist developing nations with funds to reduce CFC production. All representatives attending the conference except the U.S. delegates approved the plan. According to a report in *The Washington Post*, the decision not to take part in the aid plan was made on the advice of President Bush's chief of staff, John Sununu. EPA administrator William Reilly and other administration officials supported the idea, as did many Republicans and Democrats in Congress.[44]

Over the next few weeks, national leaders, heads of manufacturing companies, and environmental groups appealed to President Bush to adopt the fund plan. By July, when another meeting on CFC reductions was held in London, President Bush's staff announced a change of policy: the United States would contribute to the fund. American support encouraged countries such as China and India to ratify the Montreal Protocol. With rapidly growing populations, both China and India are expanding their manufacturing, and with help from the fund they now are able to seek substitutes for CFCs in manufacturing processes and in refrigeration.

The U.S. Clean Air Act also has reinforced the federal government's position on banning CFC use. The act requires that the production of CFCs and halons be phased out by the year 2000 and places curbs on some chemicals being used as substitutes for CFCs.

FINDING CFC SUBSTITUTES

After years of insisting that there was not strong enough scientific evidence to warrant reductions in CFC use, Du Pont, in 1988, decided to phase out all production of the chemicals. The company announced it would reduce its production of CFCs by at least 95 percent by the year 2000.

According to a *New York Times* report, the firm "said it was taking the action, which would go well beyond its previous commitment only to reduce output of the chemicals, because of new scientific evidence that the threat to the atmospheric ozone layer was worse than had been thought."[45]

Du Pont urged other CFC-producing companies to seriously consider the new scientific evidence presented by NASA and to help eliminate the use of ozone-depleting chemicals. The company also called for "additional global limitations" on the production and use of CFCs and noted that substitute products were being developed.

Some CFC compounds that are less harmful to the ozone layer are already on the market. The Du Pont company is producing replacements for CFC 12, the product that has commonly been used in the manufacture of foam containers for the fast-food industry and in refrigerants and air conditioners.

Researchers and engineers in the refrigeration industry are experimenting with the substitute chemicals as well as with different designs that will include improved insulation. New types of air conditioners are being developed also. An experimental air conditioner for home use combines an old technique—cooling by evaporation—and a desiccant, which is a chemical that absorbs water. As explained in a *Popular Science* article,

> *Evaporative coolers work well in dry climates: A fan draws outside air over a damp pad, where it is cooled by picking up moisture. But when the intake air is humid to start with, it can't pick up enough additional moisture to cool significantly. That's where the desiccant comes in.* [One pound (.45 kg) of the chemical solution can absorb about 5 pounds (2.25 kg) of water.][46]

Manufacturers also are redesigning air conditioners used in motor vehicles, replacing CFCs with substitute chemicals, improved condensers, fewer joints, and tighter seals and valves. In older cars and trucks, CFCs escape from air conditioners during servicing, so engineers are designing recycling systems to recover coolants rather than allow them to evaporate. Removing coolants from refrigerators and air conditioners before they are scrapped is another way to prevent the release of CFCs.

In other industries, manufacturers are developing alternative products that do not contain chlorine or bromine. For example, Petroferm, a chemical company with headquarters in Fernandina Beach, Florida, has produced Bioact EC 7, which is made from crushed orange peels and is a terpene hydrocarbon that contains no chlorine. It is being used by such companies as American Telephone and Telegraph (AT&T) to clean computer circuit boards.

Every step taken to eliminate gaseous chemicals that disrupt our earth's atmosphere is needed, say scientists and government leaders around the world. As a Canadian environmental official put it:

> *The problems of the ozone layer, of greenhouse gases and climate change, of long-range transport of acidic and toxic substances are closely interrelated. They are all problems caused by human contamination of the atmosphere—the only one we have. A new approach, a new ethic, towards discharging wastes and chemical materials into the air we all breathe must soon be adopted on an international scale. Without this we will do irreparable damage to our earthly home.*[47]

6
POISONS IN THE AIR

Few people in Bhopal, India, can forget that tragic day in 1984. A lethal gas cloud from a chemical plant spread over the city, killing more than 3,000 people and injuring tens of thousands more. Highly toxic methyl isocynate, a derivative of cyanide, had leaked from an international Union Carbide facility.

Because similar chemical plants and the headquarters for Union Carbide are located in the United States, some members of the U.S. Congress were concerned that a tragedy such as the one in Bhopal might occur in the United States. Indeed, thousands of accidental leaks or spills of toxic chemicals had occurred during the 1980s. According to an EPA report, fifteen of those accidents released poisonous substances that had the potential to cause as many deaths and injuries as those that resulted from the Bhopal leak. Fortunately, however, winds blew acute toxins away from populated areas or the leaking chemicals were in liquid form, so emergency action could be taken to contain the toxins and avert catastrophes.

In 1986, Congress passed an amendment to an earlier

toxic waste law that requires industries to inform employees about dangerous chemicals in their workplaces. Called the Emergency Planning and Community Right-to-Know Act, the 1986 amendment provides for the public's right to obtain information about dangerous chemicals being used or stored in some 30,000 industrial plants. The act also requires communities to set up plans to deal with sudden chemical disasters or with the accidental release of radioactive materials due to the malfunction of nuclear power plants or problems with the disposal of nuclear wastes.

TOXIC CHEMICAL INVENTORY

Part of the right-to-know law mandated that industrial plants across the nation publicly disclose whether they use or store any of the more than 300 chemicals listed as hazardous by the EPA. Among the chemicals are those that are highly flammable and those that cause cancer, birth defects, neurological disorders, respiratory problems, or instant death if inhaled or absorbed through the skin.

Owners and operators of facilities that release hazardous chemicals into the environment—air, water, or land—must file reports on amounts of annual emissions that are in excess of 25,000 pounds (11,250 kg). Plants employing ten or more persons full-time are required to report. The law affects not only chemical manufacturers but also such industries as food, tobacco, textile, lumber, and printing companies; paper, metal, and plastics makers; and petroleum and coal industries.

The first inventory of toxic emissions from industries was taken during 1987, and over the next year data was compiled for publication and also for computer disks and computer information networks. In March 1989, the EPA announced its findings, which showed that a total of more than 22 *billion* pounds (10 billion kg) of toxic substances were released from industries into the air, water, underground storage wells, and landfills. Of that amount, 2.7

billion pounds (1 billion kg) of toxic pollutants spewed into the air. The diagram on page 70 illustrates how poisonous gases have polluted our planet's atmosphere.

A year later, the Toxic Inventory showed that releases of toxic chemicals from industries dropped slightly, with 2.4 billion pounds (1 billion kg) entering the atmosphere.

The Chemical Manufacturers Association insists that the total numbers are misleading and that industries have stayed within the legal limits set by state and federal laws. But many environmentalists accuse industries of using the air as a toxic waste dump.

According to the EPA, Texas and Louisiana have topped the list of states emitting the greatest amounts of toxic pollutants for two years in a row. In fact, a four-county area along the Gulf of Mexico, which includes the city of Houston, Texas, has the worst toxic emissions in the nation. The sources? Oil refineries and chemical companies. The area also is known for having the state's highest death rate from lung cancer and a cancer death rate higher than the national average.[48]

Across the nation, chemical and petroleum companies belch the most pollutants into the air. Pollutants leak from storage tanks or ponds or escape from windows and ventilating systems. Metal makers and paper and plastic companies also emit large amounts of toxic pollutants into the atmosphere.

New state laws and federal regulations require many companies to clean up their acts. The 1990 Clean Air amendments stipulate that industries must install control systems that use the best available technology to cut emissions of 189 toxic chemicals. Controls must be effective enough to reduce cancer risks to nearby residents to 1 in 10,000. If this standard is not met by the year 2003, these industrial plants must shut down.

Although industrial emissions contribute considerably to the total amount of toxic air pollutants, large amounts

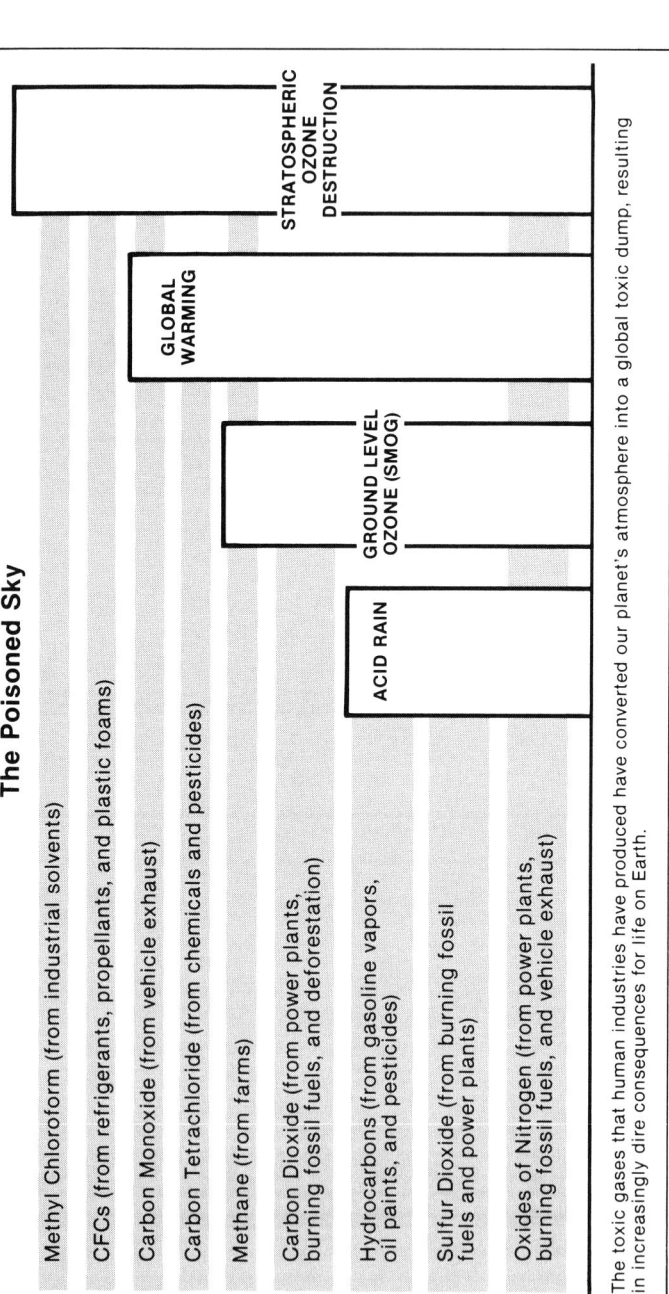

of poisonous emissions come from combined sources in a given area. For example, toxins such as perchloroethylene—used to dry-clean clothing—come from neighborhood dry cleaners. Gas stations and motor vehicles also emit toxic pollutants. The Clean Air Act requires the EPA to regulate thirty of the most toxic substances released from these and other area sources.

TOXIC EMISSIONS FROM PESTICIDES

Another source of toxic "fallout" is the widespread aerial spraying of poisonous insecticides, herbicides (weed killers and defoliants), and other pest-control chemicals, usually lumped together under the term *pesticides*. Utility companies, for example, spray herbicides to kill brush and young trees interfering with electric power lines. Government agencies spray insecticides to kill off pests that destroy trees in public parks and forests. Planes and helicopters spray chemical pesticides over farmlands and orchards, protecting crops but at the same time exposing people living nearby and workers in the fields to toxins.

Activists have been calling for the reduction of pesticide use ever since the 1960s, when Rachel Carson's book *Silent Spring* pointed out the dangers of DDT, chlordane, and other chlorine-containing pesticides made from petroleum and oil. These chlorinated substances are extremely effective in killing pests ranging from lice to termites, but the pesticides remain active for long periods, killing birds and wildlife. DDT accumulates in the soil and in the food chain and thus can be stored in human tissue as well.

DDT was banned, and chlordane and similar pesticides have been restricted. However, many toxic agricultural chemicals are still being sprayed on fields and crops. In the United States, about 2.6 million pounds (1 million kg) of pesticides are applied to farmland each year. Worldwide, pesticide use has risen steadily; sales increased tenfold, from $5 billion in 1975 to an estimated $50 billion in 1990.[49]

Yet some farmers are cutting back on pesticide sprays as well as on other agricultural chemicals. In the first place, some insects, rodents, and other pests resist chemical attacks and have adapted or even multiplied. Using large amounts of pesticides also has brought about the destruction of beneficial insects that naturally prey on pests.

In late 1989, the highly respected National Academy of Sciences (NAS) released a report showing that food production is just as high on farms that use natural methods to grow crops as on farms that rely on heavy applications of agricultural chemicals. Natural methods include efficient farm management, careful crop rotation, and integrated pest management (IPM). IPM involves biological weed and insect control, an ancient practice that basically requires monitoring pests to find out how serious the problem is, and then treating where possible with natural predators, insects that will prey on and destroy pests.

According to an NAS report summarized in *The New York Times*, the NAS believes that past federal farm policies have discouraged farmers from trying natural techniques.

> *In the Federal corn program, for instance, farmers are paid a subsidy of roughly $1 for every bushel they can produce. The incentive is to produce the most bushels. Since the end of World War II, farmers have been taught . . . that the best way to increase output is to use ample amounts of chemical fertilizer and then protect the harvest with generous applications of pesticides.*
>
> *If farm subsidies were reduced, researchers say, it is likely that farmers would no longer produce surpluses marketable only to the Government, and might encourage farmers to try natural farming techniques.*[50]

Although the majority of ranchers and farmers would not do away with all chemical pesticides, they agree that the use of agricultural chemicals could be reduced, as some farmers have done to save on the high costs of farming. More important, many farmers are concerned about the abuse of agricultural chemicals and want to cut back in order to prevent health hazards and to protect the environment.

As discussions continue on the use of toxic chemicals in agriculture, vast amounts of such substances still are sprayed on lawns and golf courses to kill weeds, insects, and other pests. Some 30 million pounds (13.5 million kg) of lawn chemicals are applied each year in the United States. Homeowners and lawn care businesses use ten times more toxic chemicals per acre than farmers use, according to the National Academy of Sciences.

Some states have passed regulations to control applications of lawn chemicals. In Maryland, for example, workers for lawn care companies must place warning signs before they treat lawns with pesticide sprays. About a dozen states have adopted similar laws, or companies have initiated the practice voluntarily. Some businesses provide "natural" lawn care or IPM methods similar to those used in agriculture.

Although not a widespread practice, nontoxic methods are replacing chemical pest-control spraying in some homes and public facilities also. You can get advice on nontoxic pest controls from the National Coalition Against the Misuse of Pesticides and many other environmental organizations (see *Organizations to Contact* in the back of this book).

POISONOUS EMISSIONS FROM WASTE

Waste disposal sites and incinerators also emit toxins into the atmosphere. The dangers of toxic waste sites came to public attention well over a decade ago with the discovery of health hazards at Love Canal, near Niagara Falls, New York. Love Canal was a dumping ground for at least 21,000 tons (18,900 tonnes) of toxic chemicals during the 1940s and 1950s. The site was filled in, as was common practice at the time, and a school was built on it. But as the years went by, toxic chemicals began seeping from the site, contaminating the air, water, and land. Trees and shrubs died, and people living nearby reported serious illnesses. Hundreds of families were evacuated from the area around Love Canal during the 1970s.

In recent years, controversy over building toxic waste incinerators has flared across the land. People object to waste burners in their communities because they do not believe the facilities are safe. Although cities often burned solid waste in the past, most municipal incinerators were shut down after federal laws banned hazardous pollutants emitted from smokestacks. Many incinerators have released poisonous heavy metals and dioxin into the atmosphere.

Dioxin compounds, which include seventy-five different species, were part of the defoliant "Agent Orange," used during the war in Vietnam. The herbicide was sprayed on plant and tree foliage that provided ambush cover for enemy soldiers. Since the war, a number of U.S. veterans groups have contended that the defoliant has caused long-term health problems (including several kinds of cancer) among those exposed. Farmers who have used herbicides with dioxin also have linked the chemical to illnesses they have suffered, such as diseases of the liver and cancer.

Manufacturers of incinerators being built today argue that air pollution control devices in burners keep toxic emissions within legal limits, and high temperatures destroy waste without producing large volumes of toxic ash. City officials say they have to have ways to dispose of waste—municipal landfills are closing because toxic substances leak from land sites and percolate through soil into water supplies. As a result, some cities have built huge incinerators, some of which turn waste into electrical power.

Nevertheless, critics contend that burning waste is not an efficient way to produce energy because of the high costs (hundreds of millions of dollars) of building the plants and installing filters and scrubbers to prevent toxic emissions. In addition, citizens are still concerned about poisonous pollutants and have organized protests to fight the building of new mass burners. Opponents of burners believe that the safest alternatives are reducing toxic waste at its source and using nontoxic materials whenever possible in manufacturing and business.

CITIZEN PROTESTS

Denis Hayes, attorney and chairman of Earth Day 1990, noted: "The most dangerous environments are in communities that are the least powerful. Poor people and minorities are downwind from the most toxic incinerators . . . in fields when pesticides are sprayed from planes . . . in factory jobs having the highest exposure to dangerous substances."[51]

Studies confirm Hayes's statements. The U.S. General Accounting Office, for example, found that most of the toxic waste sites in southeastern states were in black communities. Another study, conducted by the Council on Racial Justice of the United Church of Christ, showed that, across the nation, commercial hazardous waste facilities are located more often in areas where black or Hispanic people live than in other communities.

According to Paul Ruffins, executive editor of Black Network News, industries long have used strategies to persuade people in the work force that they should take a stand *against* environmental regulations. Ruffins points out that ever since the first Clean Air Act passed several decades ago, industries have fought back with campaigns to convince working people, especially blacks and

Hispanics, that controls on industry would mean the loss of jobs. In fact, over the years, some industries have provided funds for civil rights organizations, such as the National Association for the Advancement of Colored People (NAACP) and the Urban League, with the expectation that these groups would oppose regulations on industry, which has been the case.[52]

As people have become more aware of the health hazards of toxic substances, thousands of citizen action groups have formed across the United States. According to *Greenpeace*, "some 5,000 anti-toxics groups have in a few short years organized into the most effective challenge to business as usual that the United States has seen since the 1960s . . . the new toxics movement has crossed class, race, and geographical boundaries in its pursuit of a clean environment."[53]

Campaigns to prevent or stop pollution can be long, painful ordeals. In the first place, many citizens are not eager to fight local companies or large corporations, even when they are victims of a polluted environment. They or their relatives and friends may be employed by the very factories that emit toxic wastes. Workers fear losing their livelihood if they or others protest an employer's practices. Taking a position on one side or the other can cause friction between family members, friends, and co-workers and sometimes can divide entire communities.

Yet people become activists when they believe they or their families are in danger. Local groups sometimes seek help from such national organizations as Greenpeace and the Citizens Clearinghouse for Hazardous Waste, which began in Love Canal as one of the first community groups to fight the dumping of hazardous waste in unregulated landfills. The Environmental Research Foundation has established the computer data base RACHEL that describes the effects of toxic substances, and the National Toxics Campaign set up the first independent, public-interest testing laboratory for citizens who want to find out the chemical makeup of air, water, and waste samples. Addresses for these and other organizations are listed on page 139.

How do citizen groups get started? Usually, people who live in a neighborhood or community in which a factory or business is emitting dangerous pollutants (within legal limits or in defiance of environmental laws) begin by gathering information about the substances polluting the air. People also investigate the health or environmental hazards of contaminants. Data on hazardous emissions can be presented to a company with a request that the firm "do the neighborly thing." In other words, citizens appeal to industries to act for the benefit of the entire neighborhood or community, rather than pollute the air (or land or water) with substances that can harm everyone. If companies fail to clean up or control pollutants, citizen groups then may decide to set up action campaigns that include protest marches, letter writing to state and local regulators and the media detailing pollution hazards, and legal battles against a company.

In Louisiana, for example, citizens have conducted several marches to protest the toxic emissions from petrochemical plants along the Mississippi River. In observance of Earth Day 1990, one march took place between April 6 and April 22, starting in New Orleans and ending in Baton Rouge. Within this corridor, often called "cancer alley," people suffer a cancer rate four times higher than the national average.

Another citizen campaign began in Jersey City, New Jersey, in 1989. For many years, Jersey City and nearby towns served as sites for the manufacture of chromate chemicals that were used to make such products as photographic materials and stainless steel and to tan leather. Chromium waste from the chemical manufacturing process piled up alongside plants, creating "mountains" of yellow slag and spreading yellow chromium dust through the air, water, land, and other surfaces. Much of the waste was deposited in landfills or used to construct foundations for buildings. The neighborhood accepted the waste piles as part of the landscape—until they learned that chromium, a potent carcinogen, could be linked to the high incidence of lung cancer among young people in the community.

Citizens organized a bus trip to the state capitol in Trenton, demanding that the environmental department take action to clean up their communities. The state arranged for some chromium waste sites to be paved over as a short-term measure, but citizens said they wanted the chromium heaps removed entirely.

Although the state has funds for cleanup, officials say they want owners or operators of the chemical plants to pay the costs. That may take many more years of effort and continued pressure from citizen groups. As one member of the citizen group told a *Washington Post* reporter, "If a company is making money, sometimes they close their eyes to things that are dangerous for people."[54]

REDUCING HAZARDOUS EMISSIONS

Of course, most companies do not set out to be "bad guys," and some have started to respond to consumer demands to reduce toxic chemical emissions. Eastman Kodak in Rochester, New York, for example, has cut back annual emissions of nearly 9 million pounds (4 million kg) of toxic chemicals such as dichloromethane and formaldehyde, which have been linked to cancer. Although company officials say they do not believe emissions from their plants are human carcinogens, they also say Kodak hopes to reduce emissions by 70 percent by 1995.

Other industries also are finding ways to cut back on toxins. Monsanto, which produces chemicals for agriculture and food preservatives, says it will reduce toxic emissions from its facilities by 90 percent, by recycling some waste chemicals and using processes that generate less waste. Du Pont, Dow Chemical, Polaroid, Union Carbide, and 3M have announced cutbacks in toxic pollutants.

States, too, are taking action. Lead—a heavy metal that when inhaled or ingested can cause mental retardation, nervous disorders, and even death—is no longer used in exterior house paints and is being eliminated in interior paints manufactured in California, a state that has set strict controls on toxic emissions. A new law recently has been passed in Louisiana to regulate 100 chemicals and to reduce toxic emissions to 50 percent by 1994. Other states, such as Ohio, New Jersey, Massachusetts, and Oregon, have taken legislative steps to reduce toxic air pollutants.

Still, careful monitoring of airborne hazardous wastes from industries and other sources will continue, since chemical assaults are far-reaching. *National Wildlife* noted in its annual report on the state of the environment: "Air in the Arctic Circle, thousands of miles from any industrial plant or farm field, contains disturbing quantities of . . . toxic chemicals. By examining human remains in 500-year-old graves, researchers found that Greenland Eskimos today have three to seven times the mercury, copper, and lead their ancestors carried, an increase undoubtedly due to airborne pollutants from European, Canadian and U.S. industry."[55]

7
THE ULTIMATE POLLUTANT

Ever since World War II, when the first atom bombs were dropped, people worldwide have been concerned about the threat of nuclear explosions that could destroy the planet. Even if there were no possibility of a nuclear war, peaceful uses of nuclear power (generating electricity, for example) create apprehension. People fear exposure to high levels of radioactivity that can cause serious illnesses or instant death.

Frequently, fears stem from news reports about problems surrounding nuclear facilities. In 1979, for example, an accident at the Three Mile Island nuclear power plant in Pennsylvania was covered by news media nationwide. A valve malfunctioned, and water to cool the nuclear core in the reactor was cut back. Rather than increasing the supply of water, operators mistakenly reduced the coolant, making the problem worse and causing the core to overheat. The result was a 50 percent meltdown of the core and release of radiation.

Since the Three Mile Island accident, people across the country have debated whether the amount of radiation released has caused health problems. Some scientists expect to see increasing cases of cancer among those exposed to the radiation; other experts claim that there have been no adverse effects from the accident, nor are any expected. Countless articles, booklets, and other published materials thereafter touted the safety of nuclear reactors with assurances that no one had ever died from radiation released by a nuclear power plant.

However, another nuclear power plant accident in 1986—this one in the Soviet Union—did cause deaths. The Chernobyl nuclear plant in the Ukraine exploded, spewing particles of radioactive materials for miles. Winds and rains carried the particles across vast areas of Europe. More than thirty people were killed and hundreds more became ill, suffering from various forms of cancer.

During the late 1980s, problems with U.S. nuclear facilities on military bases came to light. Information about operations at more than a dozen weapons plants had been kept secret for more than forty years because of what federal officials called risks to national security. But federal government studies to document the health problems of workers at nuclear weapons plants revealed sloppy and sometimes illegal management practices. Among the disclosures were mechanical failures and poor waste disposal practices that led to environmental contamination as well as hazards to public health.

HOT SPOTS OF NUCLEAR WASTE

Nuclear weapons facilities are among the most polluted toxic waste sites in the nation. Highly radioactive (high-level) waste is generated from weapons-making facilities that have been in operation since World War II. The plants are located on sites across the nation, from the Hanford Reservation in the state of Washington to several facilities in Ohio to the Savannah River plant in South Carolina.

Several have been shut down for cleanup and to correct safety hazards and violations of federal environmental laws that regulate disposal of toxic chemicals and radioactive wastes. As one article in *The New York Times* explained:

> *At the Savannah River Plant . . . an emerging record of shoddy workmanship—including more than a dozen previously unreported safety mishaps—has raised concerns about the possibility of a major nuclear accident.*
>
> *And at . . . Fernald [Ohio], the Energy Department has acknowledged that for years it permitted the emission of radiation in quantities known to be harmful to public health.*[56]

One of the worst sites is the weapons-manufacturing complex known as Rocky Flats near Denver, Colorado, which makes plutonium triggers for warheads and produces wastes like plutonium dust, a lethal carcinogen. Some workers exposed to plutonium dust believe the radioactive material is linked to the cancers they now suffer. Parts of the Rocky Flat facility and other weapons plants have been shut down to clean up contaminated areas.

The aging Hanford plant was permanently closed, but high-level nuclear waste still leaks from storage tanks on the site. Some of the storage tanks buried underground contain potentially explosive gases. According to an Associated Press (AP) report in April 1990, one of the tanks "contains 1 million gallons [3.8 million liters] of mixed radioactive waste. Some wastes dumped into the tank in the 1970s contained organics, which are now decomposing and giving off hydrogen gas. The organics were used to separate radioactive strontium from other wastes before they were stored."[57]

Federal nuclear weapons plants have been supervised by several U.S. agencies over the years. But since 1977, the U.S. Department of Energy (DOE) has been overseeing nuclear weapons plants and contracting with private companies to operate the huge facilities that make atomic and hydrogen bombs and fuel for nuclear reactors on warships. When President George Bush appointed James D. Watkins secretary of the DOE, Watkins promised that the weapons plants would be more open to public scrutiny and that repairs and cleanup would be at the top of the DOE agenda.

Estimates of total costs to clean up nuclear weapons facilities have ranged from $130 billion to $170 billion. Yet in 1990, only $3.3 billion was set aside for the cleanup of the weapons plants. In contrast, $8.5 billion was allocated for the production of more nuclear weapons and for testing at the Nevada Test Site, where a bomb is exploded about once every month.[58]

WHAT TO DO WITH RADIOACTIVE WASTE?

Most high-level radioactive waste comes from spent (used) fuel rods removed from nuclear reactors. The fuel rods are narrow tubes filled with pellets of uranium that have been "enriched" with U-235, the only uranium isotope that will undergo fission, or split. Fuel rods are bundled together to form fuel assemblies that make up the core of a reactor. As atoms split to make heat, they release fragments, or fission products, that give off waves of energy (radiation), a process known as radioactive decay. The rate of decay is measured in a half-life, the time it takes for half of the atoms of an element to reach the level that is common in nature.

Fission products remain inside fuel rods. As they build up, they reduce the chain reaction and slow down the reactor. After three to four years, the spent fuel rods are pulled from the reactor and stored in pools of water to allow the radioactive materials to decay. Some of the radioactive materials disintegrate rapidly. Others have half-lives of hundreds, thousands, or even millions of years, and these highly radioactive materials are extremely hazardous.

At military facilities, spent fuel is reprocessed to extract some U-235 that remains in the rods and other materials, such as tritium and plutonium. Tritium is produced only at the Savannah River site and is shipped to other weapons plants, where it is used to increase the power of nuclear explosives. Plutonium is used to make bombs or to run nuclear reactors.

Since plutonium does not exist as an element in nature but must be processed from uranium ore, several DOE reactors are run simply to make plutonium for weapons. After extracting plutonium, a highly radioactive liquid waste is generated. The waste must be stored in steel and concrete tanks to protect people and the environment from radiation exposure.

At one time, commercial power companies processed spent fuel from their nuclear power plants. But the practice was banned in the United States because of fears that extracted plutonium might get into the hands of terrorists or other irresponsible weapons makers. Thus, since 1950, most high-level radioactive waste has been generated from military facilities—a total of over 170 million gallons (646 million liters), condensed to 100 million gallons (380 million liters). The material waits at reactor sites until it can be taken to a permanent storage place.

Meantime, however, some of the radioactive waste in storage tanks will be glassified to reduce the dangers of possible leaks. Basically, the process, which has been used in Europe and is being developed in Japan, involves separating liquid wastes from radioactive sludge. The sludge is further washed and filtered; the remaining slurry is mixed with ground glass and melted at 2100°F (1150°C), then poured into 10-foot (3-m) tall stainless steel canisters, where it becomes a solid material that looks like black onyx.

According to two researchers who have helped develop the world's largest glassification facility at the Savannah River weapons plant, "Some 6,000 to 8,000 canisters will be needed to contain the existing and projected high-level waste" at the site. The glassification process was tested during 1990 inside a reinforced concrete building with equipment that is remote-controlled. It will take at least fifteen years to glassify all of the high-level nuclear waste stockpiled at the Savannah River. From there, the glassified waste will be shipped to a permanent underground storage facility.[59]

Where will that storage site be? The place under study is near the Nevada Test Site at Yucca Mountain. Although the area is dry and appears stable, geologists question whether a nearby volcanic site that has been dormant for 20,000 years could become active again in the future. There are also concerns about whether climate will change, bringing more rainfall and a higher water table in the aquifer (the underground water supply) more than 1,000 feet (300 m) below the proposed site. Many experts believe it will be well into the next century before a decision is finally made on a disposal site.

THE NUCLEAR DEBATE GOES ON

While safe disposal of high-level radioactive waste is a major dilemma, there also are serious concerns about managing low-level radioactive materials. These include discarded clothing used by workers in nuclear power plants, some wastes from power plants, and radioactive medical debris. According to federal law, low-level nuclear wastes generated within a state must either be disposed of locally, or states must form a compact (regional group) and select a disposal site. The material may be buried in trenches or stored in concrete bunkers or buildings above ground.

Many citizens debate the safety of such procedures and do not want to be near any type of radioactive materials. Some citizen groups also oppose construction of nuclear power plants or other facilities connected with nuclear energy. In Louisiana, for example, a group called Citizens

Against Nuclear Trash (CANT) is opposing a uranium enrichment plant that would be built near Shreveport and financed by private investors. The plant would enrich uranium ore with U-235 so that it could be used as a fuel in reactors. Although investors and government officials claim the plant would pose no danger to people in the area, organizers of the citizen group say that wherever there are enrichment facilities there have been radiation hazards.

In New England, citizen groups for years blocked the licensing of Seabrook, a power plant built by a group of utility companies. Seabrook is located near the New Hampshire–Massachusetts border but has been sitting idle. In March 1990, the Nuclear Regulatory Commission, which is responsible for licensing and overseeing operations of commercial nuclear power plants, allowed Seabrook to begin producing nuclear power. Officials for the nuclear power industry believe licensing of the plant is a sign that nuclear power will be part of the overall energy strategy for the future.

However, Public Citizen, a group directed by consumer advocate Ralph Nader, points out that although some new plants were completed during the 1980s, there have been no new orders for nuclear plants in the United States since 1978. A Public Citizen report noted that "more plants were canceled or permanently retired during the past decade than were completed." (At present, there are 112 nuclear reactors generating power in the United States.) Public Citizen and some other groups, such as the Union of Concerned Scientists, the Worldwatch Institute, the Sierra Club, and Greenpeace, believe that generating nuclear energy is a high-risk technology. Such groups say that an energy policy in the United States should focus on conserving energy and developing alternative renewable energy sources, such as nonpolluting solar and wind power for generating electricity.

On the other hand, some scientists and nuclear power researchers believe that nuclear power should be included with alternative energy sources to help reduce the dependence on fossil fuels and the emissions that lead to global warming and air pollution. Paul Gray, president of the Massachusetts Institute of Technology, wrote: "Even with the prospect of solar and wind power, new nuclear power plants are going to be needed to meet energy needs and to replace the fossil fuel and nuclear plants of the 1960s and 1970s that are nearing the ends of their 30-to-40-year lives. Intensive conservation efforts must be undertaken, but they alone will not suffice."[60]

Apparently, that view is shared by DOE secretary James Watkins and others in the department. According to a report in *The Washington Post*, "The Energy Department has awarded $100 million in contracts to Westinghouse Electric Corp. and General Electric Co. to design new mid-size reactors of standardized design that would be safer and more efficient than existing facilities."[61]

HOW MUCH RADIATION IS "SAFE"?

Radiation hazards are determined by the type and amount of radiation and by the effects on human cells. Usually, the radiation dose that causes biological damage is measured by a unit called a rem. Doses of 100 to 400 rems at one time to the entire body are likely to cause serious illnesses and death. When atomic bombs were dropped on Hiroshima and Nagasaki, Japan, during World War II, victims were exposed to 1,000 rems over a short period of time—a dose that causes death immediately.

In the United States, the EPA sets limits for the radiation allowed for a total population and for an individual within that population. The radiation limit is expressed in millirems (a millirem [mrem] is $\frac{1}{1000}$ of a rem). Radiation exposure for an individual is limited to 500 mrem per year. This does not include "background radiation" from biogenic and anthropogenic sources. For example, a person receives radiation from the sun's rays, from building materials, from the earth, and from some foods. Individuals also are exposed to radiation from such anthropogenic sources as color television sets, dental and medical x-rays, luminous watches, smoke detectors, and various manufacturing processes. The "average" radiation dose from both biogenic and anthropogenic sources in the United States is about 200 mrem per year.

Certainly, there is no argument that large doses of radiation can kill or cause cancer or damage to a person's reproductive system. But there are long-standing debates about whether doses of radiation below 1 rem are health hazards. Some scientists believe that any amount of radiation over a period of time can be damaging. Others argue that there are very few risks from low-level radiation. Determining health risks and effects of small doses of radiation is complicated by the fact that other agents—poisonous chemical emissions, for example—may trigger cancer or birth defects.

8
HAZARDOUS INDOOR AIR

Radiation hazards are not limited to nuclear reactors and radioactive wastes. In recent years, Americans have been alerted to the possibility that they can be exposed to radiation in their homes—and sometimes workplaces—from radon gas, which forms naturally during the decay process of uranium in soils and rocks. As uranium decays, it becomes radium, which decays further to form radon gas. Radon can percolate through the ground and seep through cracks and floor drains in building foundations or through crawl spaces and joints. Although radon disperses outdoors, it becomes a health hazard inside the home. Radon decays into elements that attach themselves to particles of smoke and dust, which can be inhaled. Radon products continue to decay in the lungs, irradiating healthy tissues and causing cancer cells to form.

About the time radon hazards were discovered in U.S. homes (during the mid-1980s), there was increasing awareness that other substances in indoor air also could pose health risks. After a series of tests over a five-year period, the EPA found that the levels of air pollutants in some buildings are two to five times higher than levels of those same pollutants measured outdoors. In some homes tested, concentrations of toxic pollutants sometimes reached peak levels 200 to 500 times higher. Rural residents were just as likely to suffer from polluted indoor air as those living in urban homes.[62]

The situation is compounded by the fact that most people spend from 80 to 90 percent of their time inside buildings, many of which are sealed tightly to conserve energy. Airtight buildings cut heating and cooling costs but tend to increase the concentrations of indoor pollutants, resulting in what is popularly known as the "sick building syndrome."

Contaminants in homes, offices, and other buildings are posing serious health risks for millions of Americans, say medical and air pollution experts. EPA researchers believe that well over 11,000 deaths each year may be due to indoor air pollutants. Contaminants range from toxic metals and mineral fibers to hundreds of hazardous organic compounds (those that contain carbon as well as other elements) in household products such as cleaners and pesticides—a kind of "chemical soup" inside buildings.[63]

WHO'S AT RISK FROM RADON?

Although the vast majority of American homes are free of radon, at least 8 million may have high levels of the radioactive gas, according to EPA estimates. The homes most likely to be radon-prone are in areas of the nation where there are underlying deposits of uranium ore in rocks and soil. One such area, called the Reading Prong, extends from eastern Pennsylvania through New Jersey and from southern New York to Connecticut. Rocks and soils with high deposits of uranium also can be found in black shale areas of central and southern Indiana and parts of Tennessee and in the West, particularly Colorado, Wyoming, Idaho, and Montana.

Usually, people living in one- or two-story homes are more likely to be exposed to radon than those living in apartment buildings. Tests have shown that radon concentrations are highest when closest to the ground (or underground, as in a basement). The gas tends to disperse as it rises.

Yet homes built on land formations that contain uranium do not necessarily have similar concentrations of radon. Even houses located side by side or nearby in a neighborhood may not share the same levels of radon contamination. Why? Primarily because there are differences in the strength of the radioactive materials in underlying soil and variations in indoor air pressure. If the pressure of radon gas in the bedrock or soil is greater than the air pressure inside a house, the gas can be drawn indoors through small openings. Researchers have concluded that low indoor air pressure is one of the most important factors in determining the levels of radon concentration in a house.

How do you determine whether radon gas is seeping into your home? Using a fairly inexpensive testing device called a charcoal canister may be the way to begin. You can purchase such a device at a supermarket, discount, or hardware store. Place the open can in the lowest part of the house, either in the basement or on the first floor. Activated charcoal or carbon in the can absorbs radon and holds its decay products. Within a few days or a week, you can send the canister, labeled with your name and address, to a lab for testing.

Another type of device, called an alpha track detector, requires a longer time for testing—from three months to a year in one part of the house. As its name implies, the device "tracks" alpha particles that are emitted as radon decays. The particles hit polycarbonate plastic, leaving tracks or marks that can be seen only under a microscope. This device also must be sent to a lab to determine the levels of radon.

Since uranium deposits can be found in all parts of the

United States, the EPA has urged all homeowners to test for radon contamination. The agency points out that radon is the second leading cause of lung cancer deaths and that high concentrations of radon are more life-threatening than other air pollutants such as toxic emissions from industries. In spite of the wide publicity about radon hazards, however, many people still do not test for concentrations of the deadly gas. As *Consumer Reports* pointed out, people seem indifferent to a contaminant that can be avoided. "In most cases, homeowners who are living with dangerously high levels of radon can reduce it to acceptable levels for a few hundred dollars. The job rarely costs more than $1500," the magazine report noted.[64]

Even if high levels of radon cannot be reduced quickly in your home, you can lower your risks of lung cancer by spending less time in areas (such as a basement workroom or family room) with high radon concentrations. In addition, reducing exposure to tobacco smoke can reduce radon hazards since radon poses the highest risks to smokers. The EPA estimates that between 5,000 and 20,000 smokers exposed to radon die each year, compared to an estimated 3,000 deaths among nonsmokers exposed to radon.

CIGARETTE SMOKE

Whether radon is present or not, tobacco smoke, as is well known, can pollute indoor air. Tobacco smoke is said to contain an estimated 4,600 chemical compounds, some of them known carcinogens. Each year more than 300,000 deaths from such illnesses as lung cancer and heart disease are attributed to cigarette smoking.

Although the percentage of adults in the United States who smoke has dropped from 40 percent in 1965 to 29 percent today, the costs of health problems due to smoking and loss of productivity on jobs total $52 billion a year, according to Louis Sullivan, secretary of the U.S. Department of Health and Human Services.

Smokers are not the only ones facing health hazards. Nonsmokers who regularly inhale tobacco smoke (so-called secondhand or sidestream smoke) are at risk also. Adult nonsmokers living in households with smokers are 30 percent more likely to develop lung cancer than are those who live in households with nonsmokers. For children living in homes with smokers, the risk of respiratory disease is 20 to 80 percent higher than for those in nonsmoking households.[65]

Carbon monoxide is a major component in cigarette smoke and can be especially dangerous to developing fetuses, researchers theorize. Information has been widely circulated on the lethal effects of carbon monoxide from motor vehicle exhausts and faulty heating units. But only in recent years have researchers linked carbon monoxide with adverse effects on the unborn. Pregnant women who smoke risk passing on carbon monoxide to fetuses in their wombs, thereby causing learning defects in their children.

Because of health hazards, laws ban smoking in public buildings and on most airline flights within the United States. Smoking also is limited on buses, trains, and other forms of transportation. Most hospitals and other medical facilities, as well as businesses such as restaurants, limit or prohibit smoking except in special areas.

ASBESTOS

Many Americans today have heard or read about the dangers of asbestos, a natural mineral fiber. Asbestos has been used widely in the United States. Not too long ago, construction materials such as cement, floor tiles, and roofing shingles were made routinely with asbestos. The mineral also was used in insulating material for home appliances and in insulating wrap for heating ducts and water pipes. Because asbestos is a fire retardant, it became part of fire-resistant textiles. It also has high traction capabilities, which made it a valuable material for vehicle brakes.

Today, federal laws ban most uses of asbestos. The bans were prompted by studies showing that industrial workers who handled large amounts of materials containing asbestos (such as shipyard and construction workers) were victims of lung cancer. Although some asbestos can be released into water supplies that run through concrete pipes laced with the mineral fibers, airborne asbestos poses more risks. When released into the air, tiny asbestos fibers, which are like glass slivers, can be inhaled, lodging in lung tissue and leading to disease.

Asbestos materials still can be found in many older public buildings such as schools. Since an estimated 15 million students and 1.4 million workers may be exposed to asbestos in older school buildings, Congress passed a law in 1986 requiring local school districts to inspect schools and remove asbestos or seal it with a protective coating, if necessary.[66] States followed up with legislation of their own to protect citizens from contractors who use unsafe practices when removing or disposing of asbestos. Some states have tougher rules for controlling asbestos than the federal regulations.

What about asbestos in older homes? The National Asbestos Council, a group of companies certified to remove or control asbestos, says that asbestos materials pose little risk for homeowners *if* these materials are intact. However, if asbestos insulation around pipes, for example, is damaged or decaying, some fibers might be released into the air. Removing old asbestos floor or ceiling tiles, plaster, or some textured paints can release fibers also. In such cases, asbestos removal experts advise homeowners to leave the materials alone. Even vacuuming can be dangerous since the asbestos fibers seep through vacuum filters. Get professional advice and help. Most state or local environmental agencies and health departments can provide booklets or advice on asbestos, or consumers can write to the Federal Consumer Product Safety Commission (Washington, DC 20207) or call the commission's hotline (800-638-2772).

LEAD-LACED AIR AND DUST

The hazards of lead in the air (and in water) have been well documented and widely publicized. Between 1975 and 1986, more than 90 percent of the lead in gasoline was removed to prevent lead fumes from polluting the air and endangering public health. But the perils of lead poisoning still threaten many Americans in their workplaces and homes.

The federal Occupational Safety and Health Administration (OSHA) set standards in 1978 to protect workers from lead poisoning; these include periodic blood testing for employees working in areas with 30 or more micrograms of lead per cubic meter of air. But some employers do not conduct air tests, and public health researchers say that OSHA does not have enough inspectors to cover all of the industries, such as battery manufacturers and smelters, where high lead levels could threaten the health of workers.

Many older public buildings, apartments, and homes in the United States also can be sources of lead pollutants. Since water pipes in many older buildings were welded with a solder that contains lead, the metal can leach into water supplies. Lead solder has been banned, however, since 1986. Another source of the poisonous metal is lead-based paint (banned since 1977), which can chip or chalk (become like powder), releasing lead into the air. When people remodel older buildings, they often tear down walls and strip paint from woodwork, creating lead-laced dust that can be extremely dangerous.

Although adults may be poisoned by lead, children are the most likely to be harmed. Children absorb about 50 percent of the lead they ingest, while adults retain about 10 percent. An estimated 12 million children in the United States live in housing where lead paint can release toxic vapors or dust. While many of these children are poor and live in dilapidated housing, a large percentage live in older, upscale homes that have been or are being remodeled. A report to Congress issued by the U.S. Toxic Substances and Disease Registry says that 2.4 million preschool children may have dangerous levels of lead in their blood.

What is considered a dangerous level? The Centers for Disease Control has consistently lowered the acceptable level for lead in the blood. Thirty years ago, 60 micrograms (mcg) per deciliter (about 3.5 fluid ounces) of blood was allowed. Although the allowable level is now 25 mcg, some public health officials believe the acceptable level should be lowered further. Toxicologists say that young children and fetuses can be harmed by exposure to very low levels of lead. For example, levels as low as 10 to 15 mcg/dl can cause losses in intelligence, poor attention span, and difficulties with language. Medical treatments, such as chelation—cleansing the blood—can reduce lead in the blood, but any damage from lead poisoning, according to the American Academy of Pediatrics and other medical experts, is permanent.

Researchers also have found that children exposed to low levels of lead may not display any obvious symptoms. One California family learned this the hard way. After they had renovated their old house, their cat became sick. Tests revealed lead poisoning, prompting the parents to have their two young children tested. The youngsters had to be hospitalized for treatment.[67]

What can people do if they suspect that the walls in their home are covered with lead-based paint? First, paint samples can be tested to determine whether any lead exists. If lead shows up in the samples, everyone in the household needs a blood test for lead levels. Although most people have small amounts of lead in their blood, health experts can determine whether the levels are significant. Retesting also may be required to make sure that lead is not building up in a person's body.

Cleaning up lead-based paint is not a do-it-yourself job, experts say. Removing paint by scraping or stripping can disperse lead particles in the air, and lead dust will seep through ordinary filters such as those in a home vacuum cleaner. Professionals who de-lead homes usually ask residents to leave while de-leading is in process. Workers wear protective clothing and respirators when removing paint or when covering walls with materials such as plywood paneling or a paintlike material that prevents lead from seeping through. Workers also use vacuum cleaners with special filters to clean up lead dust.[68]

TOXIC HOUSEHOLD PRODUCTS

Indoor pollutants include many VOCs—carbon-based substances that easily change. One VOC is formaldehyde, a preservative and bonding agent used in many consumer and industrial products. For example, formaldehyde is used to put the "strength" or durability into wet-strength paper towels. The chemical also is used to make insulation and many pressed-wood products such as particle board, plywood, and paneling—common home construction and remodeling materials. In addition, formaldehyde emissions come from wood, gas stoves, and cigarette smoke.

Products made with formaldehyde may release toxic gases, or formaldehyde resins may break down and give off fumes. The gas dissipates over time. However, high levels of formaldehyde emissions may occur in new and remodeled homes and offices—particularly if pressed-wood products are used—and in new mobile homes where paneling, cabinets, and furniture are made from pressed-wood materials.

What are the adverse health effects of formaldehyde emissions? Respiratory problems and eye, nose, and throat irritations are common. Headaches, nausea, and fatigue are other symptoms related to formaldehyde exposure. Formaldehyde also has been linked to cancer in laboratory animals, and the EPA has classified the chemical as a probable human carcinogen.

Some people—perhaps up to 20 percent of Americans—are sensitive to low levels of formaldehyde and suffer more severe reactions than the rest of the population. Those most at risk to formaldehyde exposure include young children, the elderly, and people with chronic respiratory problems, heart disease, and allergies. Yet with good ventilation, formaldehyde levels can be reduced in buildings. In fact, the low levels of formaldehyde in most homes cause few problems for the majority of Americans.[69]

Other VOCs that pollute indoor air include trichloroethylene (TCE), benzene, and methylene chloride. TCE is a solvent used in dry cleaning and in such products as paints, varnishes, and inks. The National Cancer Institute links TCE with cancer of the liver. Methylene chloride, a known carcinogen, is a component of paint and varnish strippers. Benzene, another cancer-causing substance, is not only a component of cigarette smoke but is released from paints and varnishes and plastics as well.

Insecticides and many other consumer products that people use every day also contaminate indoor air with substances that cause respiratory ailments and disorders of the nervous system or may be responsible for birth defects. Only 2 percent of the 60,000 to 70,000 chemicals that have been introduced since World War II have been tested, so no one can be sure how a combination of substances in indoor air will affect human health.

Recently, some medical researchers have begun to recognize that an increasing number of Americans are suffering from "environmental illness," a variety of symptoms that appear to be caused by sensitivity to chemicals in the environment. The National Academy of Sciences has estimated that at least 15 percent of Americans may suffer from exposure to very small amounts of chemicals in in-

Many household products emit hazardous chemicals that pollute indoor air.

door air. Their symptoms include extreme fatigue, blurred vision, rapid heartbeat, breathing problems, confusion, dizziness, nausea, and severe stomach pains.

For years, most medical practitioners have claimed that such symptoms were due to allergies or imagined illnesses. Nevertheless, a recent report by Nicholas A. Ashford of Massachusetts Institute of Technology and Claudia S. Miller of the Health Science Center at the University of Texas concluded that scientific evidence backs up the theory of environmental illnesses. The researchers, who prepared their report for New Jersey's Department of Health, also noted that data suggest "chemical sensitivity is increasing and could become a large [economic] problem" as workers who are hypersensitive to chemicals are disabled by exposure to toxins.[70]

Some medical specialists, who call themselves clinical ecologists, theorize that a person's immune, nervous, and hormonal systems are damaged by exposure to large amounts of a toxic chemical (such as a massive dose of a pesticide) or an accumulation of small doses of toxins over a long period. Usually, the specialists suggest that patients suffering from environmental illness avoid toxic compounds, reduce stress, and improve their diet with more nutritious foods (as well as eliminating those that might cause allergies).

CLEANING INDOOR AIR

Although the majority of Americans do not seem to suffer from hypersensitivity to synthetic chemicals in indoor air, an increasing percentage of the population wants to find ways to live and work in toxin-free environments. One method is to substitute nontoxic items for those consumer goods that emit poisonous fumes or particles. Basic ingredients for nontoxic cleaners, for example, are baking soda, borax, soap, washing soda, and white vinegar. Within the past few years, many consumer magazines have carried articles on how to use these "natural" cleaners, and the environmental organization Greenpeace has produced an excellent reference booklet: "Stepping Lightly on the Earth: Everyone's Guide to Toxics in the Home" (see bibliography).

Some indoor air pollutants, such as tobacco smoke and dust particles, can be removed with air purifiers or filtering systems. But air purifiers do not trap carbon monoxide, sulfur and nitrogen oxides, or radon, according to tests conducted by Consumers Union (CU), a nonprofit organization that advises consumers about many goods and services. CU's magazine *Consumer Reports* noted that "if you have allergies, an air purifier alone probably won't help much. . . . Nor should you expect an air purifier to remove odors or dangerous gases. Such problems are best handled by controlling sources and improving ventilation."[71]

Another way to clean indoor air is with green plants, studies by the National Aeronautics and Space Administration (NASA) have shown. Since the early 1970s, NASA has been developing life-support systems for space vehicles and space stations. In the process, researchers discovered that VOCs such as formaldehyde, benzene, and TCE could be removed from indoor air with common houseplants. For example, the spider plant effectively removes formaldehyde. Other plants, such as various species of philodendrons, ivy, lilies, and the banana tree, also absorb VOCs. Scientists are not sure how plants perform their cleansing operations nor how many plants may be needed to detoxify an enclosed space. But NASA researchers suggest that one plant per square foot of living space could do the trick.[72]

9
CLEAN AIR—HOW DO WE GET IT?

Although scientists continue to study the health effects of indoor air pollutants, most research funds and federal and state programs in the United States are focused on outdoor air quality. Indeed, an estimated $32 billion per year and countless research efforts have gone into controlling many of the outdoor air pollutants described in earlier chapters. In 1990, when the U.S. Congress reauthorized the Clean Air Act, the federal law required even more stringent controls, which will cost billions of dollars more.

Yet there are many critics who point out that federal laws do not establish a comprehensive national policy to conserve energy and develop alternatives to fossil fuels. Many environmental groups say that the Clean Air Act does little to address the problems of the enhanced greenhouse effect and other global environmental concerns.

GLOBAL CONCERNS

Few industrialized countries have established national policies or programs designed to tackle global environmental problems, although some legislative actions have been taken. Finland was the first to tax carbon dioxide emissions as a means of controlling them. Taxes to combat air pollutants also have been imposed in Norway and Sweden, but companies can earn rebates or exemptions if they reduce emissions.[73]

Only recently have pollution concerns been addressed in Eastern European countries and the Soviet Union, where the environment has been sacrificed to decades of industrial growth. Cities in the Soviet Union, Poland, Hungary, Czechoslovakia, and East Germany are so polluted from industrial emissions that some waterways and land areas are considered biologically dead, unable to sustain animal or plant life.

Air pollution reportedly costs Hungarians up to $60 million per year in health problems. The life spans of people in Czechoslovakia's industrial sections, where factories spew heavy smoke and toxic fumes into the air, are fifteen years shorter than those of people in other parts of the nation. Steel mills and chemical manufacturing have so contaminated the air in Poland that many residents of such cities as Krakow suffer serious illnesses.

In Germany, factories, smelters, refineries, and power plants contaminate the air with fumes and filth. According to a report in *Science*, "power plants around Leipzig pour more dust and sulfur dioxide into the air than you'd find in any other country in Europe. In fact, 92.6% of the population of Leipzig suffers some sort of health problem caused by sulfur dioxide; 87.5% suffer a problem caused by dust."[74]

Eastern European nations and the Soviet Union are beginning to deal with their environmental ills, but they do not have the vast sums of money needed for cleanup costs. Already some financial help has come from such countries as Sweden, The Netherlands, Germany, Finland, and the United States. Hundreds of millions of dollars will be needed to refurbish factories that use equipment installed during the 1920s and 1930s and also to install scrubbers and other pollution controls in power plants. At the same time, some factories and power plants may be closed down, eliminating jobs. Since unemployment in Eastern European nations is high, some workers have said they would rather face health risks than the loss of jobs.

THE POPULATION ISSUE

One of the global concerns related to environmental problems (particularly the enhanced greenhouse effect) is the exploding world population. Cautioned an editorial in *Time* magazine: "Unless the growth in world population is slowed, it will be impossible to make serious progress on any environmental issue."[75] Denis Hayes, chairman of Earth Day 1990, put it this way: "Current population levels are undermining the biological basis for our future."[76]

The issue has been widely discussed since the publication in 1968 of *The Population Bomb*. The author, Paul Ehrlich, is a biologist who believes that an ever-increasing population will overload the earth's systems, with disastrous results. However, there are those who argue that a growing population is a benefit to a society because more people add to the resources of a nation, helping it to develop in ways that cannot be foreseen now. Also, some religious and ethnic groups and leaders of nations are adamantly opposed to any type of population control, believing that it is a form of genocide and inherently evil.

During most of human history, the number of people on earth was fairly stable, ranging between 5 million and 10 million for thousands of years. Only within the past century has world population increased rapidly. In the early 1800s, at the time of the industrial revolution, the human population totaled approximately 1 billion. By the mid-1900s, the number of people on earth had increased to 2.5 billion. That total again doubled in 1987. The world population will increase another billion by the year 2000.

Populations are not increasing at an even pace around the world; thus, the effects of more and more people are not the same everywhere. Mark Harwell, an ecologist at Cornell University, noted that there are places in the world where a "combination of no reserve food capacity, a stressed environment, and an outrageous population growth rate is leading to terrible consequences."[77]

For example, in tropical countries of southeast Asia, Africa, and South America, vast forests are being cut to provide for the basic needs of growing populations. Earning a livelihood is a more pressing concern than air pollution and other environmental hazards. Poverty forces people to concentrate on immediate needs. At the same time, investors and government officials encourage logging in order to earn income from lumber exports.

When tropical forests are destroyed, tons of carbon dioxide are released into the atmosphere, adding to the buildup of greenhouse gases from fossil fuel burning. Deforestation also disrupts rainfall patterns, causes soil to erode, and threatens many species of animals, insects, and plants. (The United States imports ingredients from rare tropical plants to manufacture one-fourth of all prescription drugs sold in the nation.)[78]

Each year in the tropics about 28 million acres (11 million hectares) of forests are cut for fuel or cleared for farming. In three to five years the soil is depleted and no longer produces good crops. Thus, more and more forest areas are cleared to provide for basic needs as populations continue to increase, adding more laborers but doing little to improve national economies.

Yet in industrialized nations such as the United States, where birthrates have fallen, people use up far more of the world's resources than do people in developing countries. Former president Jimmy Carter, who has worked with people in African and Asian nations to increase food production, put it this way:

Wichai Wonsunrasombat, a member of the Karen tribe in northern Thailand, prepares a graft from one of his mango trees so he can expand his orchard. For centuries, the Karen were slash-and-burn farmers, but tough new environmental laws to protect Thailand's diminishing forests have forced the tribesmen into a more conservative way of life.

> *It's easy to criticize the Third World for its burgeoning population, but deeply related to the problem of too many people is wasteful consumption. . . . It's sobering to me to know that each [American] consumes fifteen times as much of the world's limited resources as does the average citizen in India. . . . Perhaps, in addition to efforts directed at population control . . . we should exert some self-discipline to conserve resources.*[79]

INTERNATIONAL AGREEMENTS/PROGRAMS

Over the past decade, people and governments around the world have become more aware that we are all part of one biosphere. What happens in one part of the globe may indirectly affect another. As a result, some international efforts are helping to protect the global environment. The governments of several industrialized nations, including Japan, Canada, and the United States, as well as some private conservation groups, are paying a portion of foreign debt—money that Third World nations have borrowed from more affluent countries. In exchange, the debtor nations have agreed to preserve their tropical forests.

International reforestation programs, in which both government and private groups cooperate, also are underway. Some of these programs are joint efforts of the World Resources Institute (in Washington, D.C.) and such United Nations agencies as the Food and Agriculture Organization (FAO). Other reforestation programs involve private groups, business firms, and governments.

An example is a project initiated by Applied Energy Services of Virginia, a utility company that several years ago built a coal-fired electrical plant in Connecticut. Because the plant emits about 15 million tons (13.5 million tonnes) of CO_2 each year, the company decided to compensate by providing $2 million for a tree-planting program in Guatemala. Nearly 250,000 acres (100,000 hectares) of trees will be planted, enough to absorb the CO_2 from the Connecticut plant. The government of Guatemala, the U.S. Agency for International Development, the Peace Corps, and CARE, an international relief organization, are also supporting the project with funds and services.

International attention also is focused on other environmental concerns. For example, leaders of industrialized nations have met to discuss national policies to ban chlorofluorocarbons that deplete the ozone layer in the stratosphere. Germany and Britain are two nations that may ban CFCs by the year 2000.

In 1988, the United Nations set up the Intergovernmental Panel on Climate Change, which has convened a number of times to study the effects of global warming and what kinds of international policies should be set to deal with climate change. Many nations have called for the industrialized countries to cut carbon dioxide emissions 20 percent by 2005, which would involve reduction of fossil fuel use and energy demands.

According to officials at the Worldwatch Institute, a global environmental research organization, there are three basic ways to reduce use of fossil fuels: developing renewable sources of energy, improving energy efficiency, and expanding the use of nuclear power. However, Worldwatch rejects nuclear power as an option because of safety problems, high costs, and widespread public distrust of nuclear energy, not only in North America but also in some parts of Europe and the Soviet Union.

RENEWABLE ENERGY SOURCES

Renewable energy sources have been defined as resources that renew themselves over a relatively short period of time and include power from the sun (solar), wind, water (hydropower), the earth (geothermal), peat, and wood. Except for peat and wood, these resources usually do not produce pollutants or carbon dioxide. (Nonrenewable energy sources such as coal, oil, and natural gas come from plant and animal materials that fossilized and became part of the earth millions of years ago.)

Because of the low cost of oil and other fossil fuels over the past decade, there has been little incentive in the United States to develop renewable energy sources, which generate electricity at a higher price per kilowatt. Only 9 percent of the nation's electrical power comes from renewable sources, with hydropower (from rivers that have been dammed) providing about 4 percent of that. Geothermal, solar, and wind power produce most of the remaining portion of energy from renewable sources in the United States.

Geothermal power comes from heat in the earth's interior. The heat "leaks" and can be tapped by pumping water into the earth. As the water hits hot rocks, it forms steam that can be piped to a generating station above ground. In the United States, most of the geothermal sources that have been tapped for energy are in California.

California is also the location for most of the wind power being generated. Harnessing energy from the wind is similar to using old-fashioned windmills to pump water, except that wind machines developed to generate electricity stand much higher, some over 100 feet (30 m). They look like bizarre propeller trees whirling on grassy ridges. Thousands of the wind machines are located in three mountain passes in California, where winds rush through and turn the giant blades on top of tall towers, generating electricity for parts of the state.

Wind power provides just a small fraction of the energy demands in the United States. Research on this energy source suggests that if wind farms were developed in high-wind areas across the nation, the wind turbines could supply about 40 percent of the nation's total demand for electricity.[80]

Although the cost of solar power, like other renewable energy sources, is much higher than that of energy from fossil fuels, the number of solar energy plants is increasing as markets expand for this power source. To generate energy from the sun, photovoltaic, or solar, cells made from silicon are formed into disks or rectangles with grids (tiny conducting lines) attached. Atoms in the silicon absorb sunshine and release electrons. The free electrons collect on one surface of the cell and complete a circuit along the metal grid lines, creating an electrical current. When many cells are connected, as in flat panels on rooftops, the electricity generated can heat or cool a building. However, backup systems using conventional fuels are needed at night, during bad weather, and in the snowbelt areas, where the sun is often obscured during the winter months.

Another type of solar power is called the solar-thermal method, and it is being developed in California's Mojave Desert by Lutz International of Los Angeles. In this type of generating system, the sun heats oil inside pipes to a high temperature that in turn heats water, changing it into steam that generates electricity. To take full advantage of solar radiation, the pipes are inside troughs that can be raised or lowered to follow the sun's path. At night, natural gas is burned to produce electricity. Developers at Lutz say that power plants using solar-thermal methods and natural gas will be able to compete with the price of electricity generated from fossil fuels.[81]

Peat, which is plant matter that has partly decayed, is another renewable energy source—it accumulates at about 1.3 tons per acre (3 tonnes per hectare) per year. When thoroughly dried, peat can be burned as fuel. In fact, fires have started spontaneously in some peat bogs. For many years, people in Finland, Ireland, and the Soviet Union have used peat as a heating fuel, but in the United States peat has been used primarily to enrich farmlands and gardens. Then, in 1989, the first power plant using peat to generate electricity began operating in Maine. The Down East Peat Company operates the plant, which provides electricity for customers hundreds of miles away in the suburbs of Boston. Since peat does produce some sulfur, limestone scrubbers have been installed to remove the sulfur before burning.

What role will renewable energy resources play in the future? The experts vary widely in their predictions. But in general, there seems to be a consensus that although the technology is available to produce energy from sources other than fossil fuels, more research and development are needed to generate such energy at affordable prices. Also, if environmental hazards from fossil fuel combustion increase as projected, these pressures may force more concerted efforts to make use of solar, wind, and other nonpolluting energy sources. Yet more *efficient* use of energy must go along with generating power from renewable sources, the experts insist.

ENERGY EFFICIENCY

"Over all, energy efficiency improvements worldwide between 1990 and 2010 could make a 3,000,000,000-ton difference in the annual amount of carbon being released into the atmosphere. . . . There is simply no other approach that offers as large an opportunity for limiting carbon emissions," wrote the Worldwatch officials in an article published by the magazine *USA Today*.[82]

Similar views have been expressed by other writers published in a wide range of nationally distributed magazines, from *Audubon* to *Consumer Reports* to *Scientific American*. Dozens of recently published books on "saving the planet" also include sections on the need for using energy efficiently and developing renewable sources of energy (and how to accomplish these tasks). Some of these sources are listed in the Source Notes and Bibliography.

In an interview published in *Orion Nature Quarterly*, energy expert Amory Lovins noted that "the inefficient use and misuse of energy has so many side effects that just by using energy in a way that saves you money, you help solve many environmental and social problems." As the head of the Rocky Mountain Institute, Old Snowmass, Colorado, Lovins and his staff research and advise on ways to conserve energy. He explained: "By saving oil, or natural gas that can replace oil, we can profitably eliminate U.S. oil imports, while reducing acid rain, global warming, urban smog, marine spills, and many other impacts."[83]

Energy efficiency is essential if the United States is to compete successfully in global markets, according to EPA administrator William Reilly. He wrote: "It's no coincidence that our principal economic challengers, Japan and [formerly] West Germany, produce less waste and consume less energy than we do. . . . Japan now uses one-third as much energy per capita as the United States. Between 1973 and 1984, as Japan began to clean up its historic legacy of pollution and to emerge as a global economic power, the energy and raw materials used in Japanese production decreased, astoundingly, by 40 percent."[84]

What are some ways that energy can be used more efficiently in the United States? One of the most obvious is to manufacture motor vehicles that use less fuel.

A number of engineers have pointed out that automobile engines could be designed to get many more miles per gallon. Henry "Smokey" Yunick, a builder of race car engines and contract engineer for automakers, noted in a *Popular Science* interview that engines for passenger cars could get "from 50 to 70 mpg [80–112 km per 3.8 l] . . . weigh only about 150 pounds [67.5 kg] and be able to meet all planned emissions standards. There's no reason this engine couldn't be in mass production in the year 2000. All of the technology is available now."[85]

According to *Consumer Reports*, "If fuel-efficiency requirements were increased to [just] 45 mpg [72 km per 3.8 l] by the year 2000, Americans would burn 16.8 billion fewer gallons [64 billion liters] of gasoline per year." The magazine editors also suggest improving fuel efficiency by "switching to more compact engines, replacing heavy steel parts with plastics, and improving automatic-transmission design." Other measures would include higher gasoline taxes to encourage conservation and to promote expanded and improved public transportation systems and more research on renewable sources of fuel. U.S. gasoline taxes are about one-half the gas tax that other industrialized nations impose.[86]

Another energy-saving measure is to replace older household appliances with those that are better insulated and use less electrical power or fuel. In the United States, manufacturers of appliances such as dishwashers, refrigerators, water heaters, and furnaces are producing goods that meet energy-efficiency standards set by the federal government. As consumers buy new appliances, they could save a reported 30 trillion watt-hours of energy by 1995.[87]

Since lighting needs account for one-fifth of all electricity consumed in the United States, using more efficient light bulbs can reduce not only energy use but also the total emissions of air pollutants and carbon dioxide. An increasing number of consumers are replacing "regular" incandescent light bulbs with the newer compact fluorescent bulbs. Unlike the long fluorescent tubes used in businesses, schools, and other public buildings, compact fluorescent bulbs screw into most light fixtures and lamps. (They are not recommended for covered fixtures, however, and do not fit small lamps.)

Changing the type of light bulb may seem an insignificant action, but a compact fluorescent bulb uses about 25 percent less energy than a regular light bulb. A fluorescent bulb that generates the same amount of light as a 60-watt bulb costs much more than the regular bulb but lasts up to 10,000 hours (compared to about 750 hours for the 60-watt).[88]

According to the EPA, one of the most important ways to reduce the amount of energy consumed involves eliminating waste in heating and cooling buildings. Energy-efficient buildings also save money. For example, large commercial buildings with windows coated to prevent heat from escaping through the glass can save thousands of dollars in heating costs during a year. Although many residences and businesses have been "buttoned up," many more buildings need to be better-insulated and sealed to prevent energy loss, the experts say.

10
THE BUCK STOPS HERE

In a special editorial in honor of Earth Day 1990, EPA administrator William Reilly wrote that "What government and industry can achieve by way of conserving energy, slowing the generation of waste or reducing the emission of gases that cause ozone depletion and climate change, will depend to a great extent on people's readiness to change their habits, to buy new products and to safeguard nature from their own practices."[89]

People around the world seem to share that view as they express their concerns about air pollution and also about the threats to our water and land. A recent *Washington Post*-ABC News survey of more than 1,000 adults found that although "44 percent of respondents believed that polluting companies were most to blame for endangering the nation's environment, 27 percent thought apathetic citizens were most at fault."[90]

The message that some environmental organizations have been spreading in recent years is that consumers worldwide cannot "pass the buck" and expect others—governments and industries, for example—to take all of the responsibility for cleaning up our act. Solving large-scale problems requires countless individual actions. Officials of Worldwatch Institute wrote: "Our values, choices, and behaviors shape social and political change. Unless more of us join the effort, there is little hope of halting the planet's deterioration."[91]

Hundreds of do's and don'ts to help preserve the health of the earth have been published. Many of the suggestions have to do with preventing increases in air pollutants and gases that contribute to the greenhouse effect and depletion of the ozone layer in the stratosphere. Some ideas were included in previous chapters. The tips and examples of action programs that follow have been summarized from some of the resources listed at the end of this book and many other ideas presented in the printed and electronic media.

SAVING ENERGY

Some broad-based energy conservation measures have been described. But what can *you* do today, or within a short time, to save energy? Here are just a few ideas:

- Turn off lights when they are not in use.
- Use compact fluorescent light bulbs.
- Walk or ride a bike on short trips.
- Use public transportation whenever possible.
- Close off unused rooms to conserve heat or air-conditioning.
- Adjust the thermostat a few degrees lower for heating and higher for cooling to save fuel.
- Clean furnace and air-conditioner filters for better efficiency.
- Run the washer, dryer, and dishwasher only when full.

Even if you have read or heard these tips before, they are worth repeating because they are effective. For exam-

Getting out old bicycles and leaving motor vehicles in the garage is one way that people of almost any age can cut back on the use of fossil fuels and the emission of air pollutants.

ple, if you replace a regular light bulb with a compact fluorescent bulb, you keep $\frac{1}{2}$ ton (.45 tonne) of carbon dioxide out of the atmosphere over the bulb's useful life.[92] Just turning a room air conditioner off for an hour prevents the release of about 4 pounds (1.8 kg) of carbon dioxide. Reducing the use of a clothes dryer by an hour cuts carbon emissions by 10 pounds (4.5 kg).

Yet it is possible to cancel out a single conservation effort with excesses in other uses of energy, such as traveling many miles in a gas-guzzling car. In short, being consistent is an important factor in energy conservation—cut back consumption of fossil fuels wherever and whenever possible.

PLANTING/PRESERVING TREES

"If you want to fight air pollution, go plant a tree," is the title of an article in the *Smithsonian*.[93] The article, one of a dozen in a special issue dealing with the environment, describes several successful tree-planting programs. An example is TreePeople, which Andy Lipkis initiated in Los Angeles more than twenty years ago. At age fifteen, Andy was concerned about dying trees in the Los Angeles National Forest. Ozone and other gases in urban smog were killing the trees. He organized 20,000 young people to plant saplings that would resist smog. Since that ambitious beginning, Lipkis and TreePeople have initiated projects for planting millions of trees, not only in Los Angeles but also in communities around the world.

Many TreePeople projects, like tree-planting efforts of other groups, are carried out with the help of Global ReLeaf of the American Forestry Association. A national education, action, and policy campaign, Global ReLeaf was established to "improve the earth's environment through more and better trees and forests." As a Global ReLeaf brochure with the motto "Plant a Tree, Cool the Globe" points out, trees can conserve energy by shading buildings (cutting air-conditioning use) and by acting as windbreaks (reducing use of fuel for heating). One of the main goals of Global ReLeaf is to plant at least 100 million trees in U.S. cities and towns. The effort could reduce carbon dioxide emissions by 33 million tons (30 million tonnes) and save $4 billion in energy costs each year. (Instructions on how to plant a tree and a list of ways showing how trees can help solve air pollution are found on page 119.)

Who gets involved in Global ReLeaf campaigns? People in many areas of the United States and from a variety of age groups and economic backgrounds. Thousands of young people are taking part in tree-planting efforts, some of which tie in with international programs. Global Forests, for example, is sponsored by the St. Louis Area Global ReLeaf and K.I.D.S., an international student group actively involved in environmental programs. Young people in St. Louis and six "sister cities" in Italy, France, Germany, Ireland, China, and Japan are finding common bonds as they plant trees in their respective communities.

A group of fifth graders at Jackson Elementary School in Salt Lake City, Utah, initiated "Leaf It to Us," a program to promote tree planting at schools around the state. In Tucson, Arizona, elementary school students have taken part in Trees for Tucson, a Global ReLeaf program that has a goal to plant 500,000 trees that can adapt to the desert climate. High school and college students from Florida and the Carolinas to California and Oregon have started tree-planting programs.

Major companies also are involved in Global ReLeaf efforts. Amway Corporation, Atlantic Richfield Company, E. & J. Gallo Winery, McDonald's, Safeway Stores, and Texaco are examples. When McDonald's announced its national program on Earth Day 1990, the firm said it would pass out seedlings and educational materials designed to encourage people to plant 8 million trees within the next few years.

Other types of organizations working around the world

How to Plant a Tree

1. Locate a clear, open site for your tree, with generous rooting area and good drainage.
2. Loosen and blend the soil in the entire planting area 6-0 inches deep. In the center, dig a hole at least as wide, but only as deep as the root ball.
3. Remove tree from burlap or container and place on solidly packed soil so that the root collar (where the tree's main stem meets the roots) is slightly above the surrounding grade.
4. Backfill hole and lightly pack the soil into place around the tree.
5. Spread a 2-3 inch layer of mulch in the entire area, keeping a 6-8 inch distance from the tree trunk.
6. Stake tree so that it can flex in the wind. Attach stake to tree using discarded rubber innertubes. Remove them after six months.
7. Water thoroughly, but do not flood the hole. Water twice a week during dry periods.

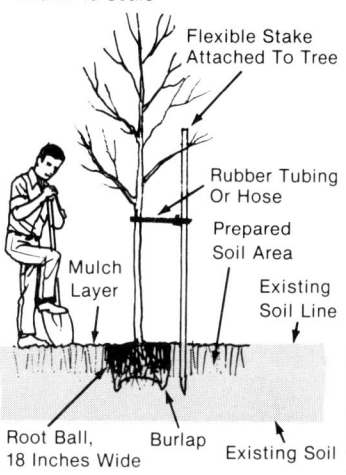

Drawn to Scale

How Trees Improve the Environment:

- Trees use carbon dioxide in the atmosphere and turn it into life-giving oxygen.
- Trees clean up the air and reduce the greenhouse effect.
- Trees help conserve energy. Three properly-planted trees around your home can cut your air-conditioning bill by 10-50 percent, and windbreaks can considerably reduce heating costs.
- Trees help turn urban "heat islands" into cool and comfortable "oases." Shading expanses of pavement with trees keeps temperatures lower and dramatically reduces energy use.
- There are at least 100 million energy-efficient tree planting sites available around homes and in America's towns and cities. Planting those 100 million trees could offset carbon dioxide emissions by 33 million tons a year, saving American consumers $4 billion each year in energy costs!
- Trees and forests filter air pollution, provide wildlife habitat, protect watershed areas, prevent soil erosion, and reduce noise pollution.
- Well-managed forests produce hundreds of products we use in everyday life, as well as a variety of recreational opportunities.
- Healthy tropical forests support over 50 percent of the world's tree and plant species, produce valuable medicines, and affect the global climate.

Source: *Global Releaf*, A Program of the American Forestry Association, Washington, D.C.

also encourage tree planting or forest preservation. One such group is CARE, an international relief and development organization that has worked with the World Wildlife Fund (WWF). CARE projects usually begin as efforts to fight poverty and hunger in developing countries. Until recent years, this goal did not necessarily jibe with conserving trees and forests. As Joseph Torres, one of CARE's agricultural experts in Africa, put it: "The farmers I work with in Uganda are so poor they barely manage to survive between harvests while right next to them is a forest full of lumber and firewood and maybe even gold. It's hard to tell them to leave the rain forest alone when it could provide lifesaving resources."[94]

However, Torres explained that he soon became a conservationist. As farmers in Uganda cleared the forestlands, they found that local springs ran dry. Why? Because rain forests are like giant sponges, soaking up rainwater and then slowly releasing it.

Over the years, CARE projects helped farmers improve agricultural methods so that they could increase crop production on less land. The farmers no longer had to cut down vast areas of forests to meet basic needs. At the same time, the World Wildlife Fund, working with CARE, helped people manage forests by controlling the number of trees cut for lumber and by planting two new seedlings for every tree cut.

Projects that combine both development and conservation also are under way in Latin America. A number of private environmental groups and some national government agencies provide funds to protect rain forests, and CARE frequently helps develop programs that take into account people's immediate needs as well as the need to conserve forests for global well-being.

BE A "GREEN" CONSUMER

"Green consuming" or buying "green" products is a relatively recent strategy that has been suggested for individual action. What is green consuming? In brief, it is buying or using goods and services that do not harm the air, water, or land. According to several national polls, a large majority of Americans refuse to buy products or pay for services that contribute to environmental problems.

However, it is not a simple matter to determine which product or company is "environmentally friendly." Advertisers often market their goods and services as nonpolluting, but some of their claims can be highly misleading. For example, some automobile manufacturers have advertised their cars as pollution-free, emitting only "harmless carbon dioxide." Yet, as many people know, carbon dioxide is one of the gases contributing to the enhanced greenhouse effect. Other car companies point out in ads that they have reduced emissions and increased the fuel efficiency of their cars—true statements. The ads do not tell you that automobile manufacturers long resisted any efforts to pass laws mandating pollution controls on cars.

In some advertisements, chemical manufacturers are taking credit for helping to inform the public about the kinds of chemicals being produced, used, or stored in factories or other businesses. The ads are factual, but not all companies provided this information voluntarily. The right-to-know laws (described in Chapter 6) *require* chemical companies to release such information.

Although more and more manufacturers around the world are jumping on the "green" bandwagon, there is help for consumers who want more than hype or advertising pitches that may contain half-truths. In most Western nations, environmental groups or government agencies have set up programs to identify products that do not harm the environment. One of the first was set up by Germany's environmental agency. The agency uses a "Blue Angel" logo to label environmentally safe products in several categories. In Canada, products that carry an ecologo with three doves and three maple leaves, representing cooperation between industry, government, and society, are considered hazard-free. Recently, the Alliance for Social Responsibility in New York City launched a Green Seal program, placing its seal on "earth-safe" products sold in the United States. Several major discount store chains, such as Wal-Mart and K-Mart, are selling a line of products that carry a "green" sticker or label.

One of the best guidebooks on "buying green" is *Shopping for a Better World* by the Council on Economic Priorities (Ballantine). It lists information about company practices that affect the environment. Other helpful guides include *The Green Consumer* by John Elkington, Julia Hailes, and Joel Makower (Penguin) and *The Green Lifestyle Handbook* edited by Jeremy Rifkin (Henry Holt). These books are listed in the bibliography.

GETTING INVOLVED

One of the most important spin-offs of getting involved in efforts to protect air quality (and the environment as a whole) is a subtle but growing change in attitudes and habits. For example, you might plan to go to the corner quickmart but decide to walk or go by bike instead of using the family car. You might be ready to zap a bug with a toxic pesticide but decide to use a nonpolluting method instead.

Of course, no one person alone can prevent global warming, or depletion of the ozone layer, or acid rain damage, or smog alerts. Nevertheless, it takes only one person to plant a tree, to turn off lights, to write a letter to a government official, or to make a decision about what kinds of products to buy and use. Many such actions taken collectively lead to changes. The point for all of us is to try to avoid being part of the problem and instead be part of the solution to cleaning up air pollution and other environmental ills.

Astronaut Kathy Thornton, in a special Earth Day issue of *New Age Journal*, explains how she felt after viewing earth from space. Her words emphasize our individual roles as caretakers of the global environment: "I don't think the Earth cares what we do to ourselves. It's up to us to care what we do to our ourselves. If we make ourselves extinct, then some other life forms will come up and they'll be the tenants in charge here. If we want to stay here, we have to make it a place where we can thrive.''[95]

GLOSSARY

Acid rain—wet or dry deposits of acidic substances.
Algae—simple plants that usually grow in water.
Anthropogenic—produced by humans.
Aquifer—an underground formation capable of storing water.
Biogenic—naturally produced.
Catalytic converter—a device that reduces emissions of pollutants from motor vehicles.
CFCs—chlorofluorocarbons; gases used in refrigeration and in various manufacturing processes.
CO—carbon monoxide; a gas formed when fuels are burned in areas with low oxygen levels.
CO_2—carbon dioxide; a colorless gas that is part of air and is released from living things.
Dioxins—a group of chemical compounds that form during manufacturing or burning of waste products.
EPA—Environmental Protection Agency.
Eutrophication—the process by which a body of water is enriched with nutrients so that it fills with aquatic plants and is low in oxygen.
Evaporation—the process of liquid changing to vapor.
Fossil fuel—fuel such as oil and coal that comes from decayed matter.

Greenhouse effect—process by which gases in the atmosphere hold heat, which could lead to global warming or increases in overall global temperatures.
Herbicide—poisonous substance used to kill weeds and other vegetation.
Hydrocarbons—substances or compounds made up of hydrogen and carbon.
Isotopes—varied atoms of the same element, but with different atomic weights or number of neutrons in their nuclei.
Leach—to extract, such as to remove substances from soil as water seeps through.
Malignant—abnormal growth.
NASA—National Aeronautics and Space Administration.
Nitrogen—a colorless, odorless gas that is part of air.
NO_x—nitrogen oxides; gases that contribute to the formation of acid rain.
Ozone layer—a layer of gas in the stratosphere that shields the earth from ultraviolet rays of the sun.
Particulates—microscopic particles made up of dust, soot, and chemical compounds; a component of smog ozone.
pH—potential hydrogen; a measurement that expresses the acidity of a water solution.
Photochemical—having to do with a chemical reaction caused by solar radiation or light.
Photosynthesis—process by which plants use solar energy to make food from carbon dioxide and water vapor.
Plutonium—a radioactive element produced in nuclear reactors.
Precursor—a forerunner; something that precedes.
Radiation—energy released in the form of particles or waves.
Radon—a radioactive gas.
SO_2—sulfur dioxide; gas that forms during the burning of fossil fuels, contributing to acid rain.

SPM—solid particulate matter; tiny invisible particles in the air.
Stratosphere—a layer of air about fifteen miles above the surface of the earth.
Strontium—a highly reactive element; the isotope strontium-90 is used in electrical power plants and is a radiation hazard.
Troposphere—a layer of air close to the earth.
VOCs—volatile organic compounds; changeable gases.

SOURCE NOTES

Chapter 1

1. Robert E. Norton, "Yes, They Mind If We Smoke," *U.S. News & World Report*, 25 July 1989, 43.
2. "We Fouled Our Nest," *Newsweek*, 22 January 1990, 66.
3. Charles Gordon, "When the Heavens Turned Yellow," *Macleans*, 25 July 1988, 38.
4. Glenn Collins, "On Not Going Up in Smoke," *The New York Times*, 29 October 1989.
5. Denise Kalette and Rae Tyson, "Air, Treated Like an 'Open Sewer,'" *USA Today*, 31 July 1989, 5B.
6. Kirk R. Smith, "Air Pollution: Assessing Total Exposure in the United States," *Environment*, October 1988, 12.
7. "Monitoring the Global Environment: An Assessment of Urban Air Quality," excerpts from the GEMS report in *Environment*, October 1989, 10.
8. Otto Friedrich, "Scrubbing the Skies," *Time*, 16 April 1990, 20-21. Also Marlene Cimons, "Car Fumes Linked to High Medical Costs," *Los Angeles Times*, 20 January 1990, A18.

Chapter 2

9. Philip H. Abelson, "Rural and Urban Ozone," *Science*, 23 September 1988, 1569.
10. Nancy Stauffer, "New Predictions on Ozone Pollution," *Technology Review*, 13.
11. Chart: "Our Dirty Air," *U.S. News & World Report*, 12 June 1989, 52.

12. Kathlyn Gay, *Ozone* (New York: Franklin Watts, 1989), Chapter 2.
13. Peter B. Reich and Robert G. Amundson, "Ambient Levels of Ozone Reduce Net Photosynthesis in Tree and Crop Species," *Science*, 1 November 1985, 566–570.
14. CNN news report, 9 March 1990.
15. "Particulate Levels Added to Times' Daily Smog Report," *Los Angeles Times*, 2 February 1990, B8.
16. "Air Pollution," U.S. General Accounting Office briefing report to Congress, January 1988, 13.
17. Philip E. Ross, "Clean-Air Fuels for the '90s," *Popular Science*, January 1990, 50.
18. "Fill 'er Up, Please—with Hydrogen," *Newsweek*, 5 March 1990, 42.

Chapter 3

19. "Acid Rain," *National Wildlife*, 3 February 1987, 8.
20. "Monitoring the Global Environment: An Assessment of Urban Air Quality," *Environment*, October 1989, 10.
21. Office of Technology Assessment, *Acid Rain and Transported Air Pollutants: Implications for Public Policy*, June 1984, 208–209.
22. As reported by Jon R. Luoma, "Acid Murder No Longer a Mystery," *Audubon*, November 1988, 130–132.
23. Don Hinrichsen, *The Earth Report* (Los Angeles: Price Stern Sloan, 1988), 66.
24. Janet Raloff, "New Acid Rain Threat Identified," *Science News*, 30 April 1988, 276.
25. James J. Mackenzie and Mohamed T. El-Ashry, "Ill Winds: Air Pollution's Toll on Trees and Crops," *Technology Review*, April 1989, 65–71; Volker A. Mohnen, "The Challenge of Acid Rain," *Scientific American*, August 1988, 30–38; Larry Kahaner, "'Creeping Degradation' Joins the List of Threats to the Nation's Parks and Forests," *Wilderness*, Winter 1988, 19.
26. Patricia Irving et al., "Productivity of Field-Grown Soybeans Exposed to Acid Rain and Sulfur Dioxide Alone and in Combination," *Journal of Environmental Quality*, October–December 1981, 478.

Chapter 4

27. James R. Udall, "Turning Down the Heat," *Sierra*, July/August 1989, 32. Also Senator Albert Gore, Jr., "Seizing the Interna-

tional Environmental Initiative," *Harvard International Review*, Summer 1990, 25–27, 61.
28. Christopher Flavin, "Slowing Global Warming," *American Forests*, May/June 1990.
29. Arthur Fisher, "Global Warming: Part 2, Inside the Greenhouse," *Popular Science*, September 1989, 67.
30. As quoted in Jerry Bishop, "New Culprit Is Indicated in Greenhouse Effect: Rising Methane Level," *The Wall Street Journal*, 24 October 1988, 1.
31. William Booth, "Action Urged Against Global Warming: Scientist Appeal for Curbs on Gases," *Washington Post*, 2 February 1990, A4.
32. Stephen H. Schneider, "Doing Something about the Weather," *World Monitor*, December 1988, 32.
33. Richard Monastersky, "Satellites Find No Global Warming in 1980s," 31 March 1990, 197.
34. Roy W. Spencer and John R. Christy, "Precise Monitoring of Global Temperature Trends from Satellites," *Science*, 30 March 1990, 1558–1562.
35. Lester R. Brown, Christopher Flavin, and Sandra Postel, "A Global Plan to Save Our Planet's Environment," *USA Today*, January 1990, 30.
36. Leslie Roberts, "Global Warming: Blaming the Sun," *Science*, 24 November 1989, 992–993.
37. From Patrick Bedard, "Change the Weather," *Car and Driver*, December 1989, 16.
38. Donella H. Meadows, "In Global-Warming Debate, Skeptics Corral Bush with a Policy of Inaction," *Los Angeles Times*, 11 February 1990, M3.
39. William K. Stevens, "Governments Start Preparing for Global Warming Disasters," *The New York Times*, 14 November 1989, C1.
40. John H. Gibbons, Peter D. Blair, and Holly L. Gwin, "Strategies for Energy Use," *Scientific American*, September 1989, 136–143.

Chapter 5

41. Richard A. Kerr, "Ozone Destruction Closer to Home," *Science*, 16 March 1990, 1297.
42. Alan S. Miller and Irving M. Mintzer, *The Sky Is the Limit: Strategies for Protecting the Ozone Layer*, Research Report No. 3, Washington, D.C.: World Resources Institute, November 1986, 12.

43. Daniel J. Dudek and Michael Oppenheimer, "The Implications of Health and Environmental Effects for Policy," in *Effects of Changes in Stratospheric Ozone and Global Climate* (Washington, D.C.: Environmental Protection Agency, 1986), Vol. 1, *Overview*, 371.
44. Michael Weisskopf, "Administration Defends Resistance to Plan for Helping Third World Cut CFCs," *The Washington Post*, 10 May 1990, A21.
45. Philip Shabecoff, "Du Pont to Halt Chemicals That Peril Ozone," *The New York Times*, 25 March 1988, A1 and A20.
46. V. Elaine Gilmore, "Clean-Air Home Air Conditioner," *Popular Science*, July 1990, 59.
47. James P. Bruce, "Man's Impact on Earth's Atmosphere," in *Effects of Changes in Stratospheric Ozone and Global Climate* (Washington, D.C.: Environmental Protection Agency, 1986), Vol. 1, *Overview*, 51.

Chapter 6

48. Rae Tyson and Julie Morris, "A First Peek Behind the Plant Gates," *USA Today*, 31 July 1990, 1A.
49. Chris Wille, "Vital Statistics," *National Wildlife*, February–March 1990, 33.
50. Keith Schneider, "Science Academy Says Chemicals Do Not Necessarily Increase Crops," *The New York Times*, 8 September 1989, 1.
51. Denis Hayes, "Earth Day 1990: Threshold of the Green Decade," *Natural History*, April 1990, 69.
52. Paul Ruffins, "Divided We Fall," *New Age Journal*, March/April 1990, 45–47.
53. Judy Christrup and Robert Schaeffer, *Greenpeace*, January/February 1990, 14.
54. Laurie Goodstein, "An Awakening to Toxic Waste: Citizens Mobilize Against Longtime Chromium Hazard in New Jersey," *The Washington Post*, 17 September 1989, A3.
55. Peter Steinhart, "Innocent Victims of a Toxic World," *National Wildlife*, February–March 1990, 22.

Chapter 7

56. Douglas Jehl, "Two Towns Share Flawed Nuclear Plants, Little Else," *The New York Times*, 12 February 1989, 25.
57. Nicholas K. Geranios, "Strange Brew Cooking in Nuclear Waste Storage Tanks," Associated Press, 1 April 1990.

58. Peter Gray, "Will the Department of Energy Finally Stop Nuking America?" *The Washington Monthly*, April 1990, 39.
59. George Wicks and Dennis Bickford, "Doing Something About High-Level Nuclear Waste," *Technology Review*, November/December 1989, 54.
60. Paul E. Gray, "We Need Safer Smaller Simpler Reactors," *Popular Science*, April 1990, 76.
61. Thomas W. Lippman, "Analyses Indicate National Consensus on Nuclear Power Is Far from Resolved," *The Washington Post*, 4 January 1990, A7.

Chapter 8

62. As reported by Larry B. Stammer, "Indoor Air—How Clean Is It?" *The Washington Post*, 23 January 1990, Z17.
63. Kathlyn Gay, *Silent Killers: Radon and Other Hazards* (New York: Franklin Watts, 1988) Chapter 1.
64. "Radon: The Problem No One Wants to Face," *Consumer Reports*, October 1989, 623–625.
65. As reported by Scott Riddle, "The Hidden Menace: Indoor Pollution," *USA Today* (Magazine), September 1989, 45.
66. Statistics from the EPA, cited in Scott Riddle, "The Hidden Menace: Indoor Pollution," 46.
67. As reported by Maura Dolan of the *Los Angeles Times* in *The Washington Post*, 10 August 1989, T11.
68. Stephanie Pollack, "Solving the Lead Dilemma," *Technology Review*, 22 October 1989, 22–31.
69. Consumer Federation of America, "Formaldehyde" (undated brochure).
70. As quoted by Michael Weisskopf, "Hypersensitivity to Chemicals Called Rising Health Problem," *The Washington Post*, 10 February 1990, A2.
71. "Air Purifiers," *Consumer Reports*, February 1989, 88–93.
72. Janet Marinelli, "Plants for Healthier Homes," *Garbage: The Practical Journal for the Environment*, March/April 1990, 36–43. Also Becky Gillette, "The Clean Green Machine," *Home Mechanix*, November 1989, 56–59.

Chapter 9

73. Leslie Jay, "A Global Call for Action," *Management Review*, June 1990, 36–37.
74. Jeremy Cherfas, "East Germany Struggles to Clean Its Air and Water," *Science*, 20 April 1990, 295–296.

75. "Planet of the Year," *Time*, 2 January 1989, 65.
76. Denis Hayes, "Earth Day 1990 Threshold of the Green Decade," *Natural History*, April 1990, 70.
77. Quoted by Arthur Fisher, "Saving the Planet," *Popular Science*, October 1989, 98.
78. Sandra Postel, "Global View of a Tropical Disaster," *American Forests*, November/December 1988, 25-29, 69-71.
79. Jimmy Carter, "The Third World Is Not a Hopeless Place," *New Age Journal*, April 1990, 132.
80. Arthur Fisher, "Saving the Planet," 92.
81. James R. Chiles, "Tomorrow's Energy Today," *Audubon*, January 1990, 61-65. Also John H. Gibbons et al, "Strategies for Energy Use," *Scientific American*, September 1989, 139.
82. Lester R. Brown, Christopher Flavin, and Sandra Postel, "A Global Plan to Save Our Planet's Environment," *USA Today* (Magazine), January 1990, 30.
83. "The Challenge Now" (interviews), *Orion Nature Quarterly*, Winter 1990, 45.
84. From William K. Reilly, "A World in Our Hands," *The Washington Post*, 22 April 1990, B1.
85. "Say, Smokey: What's the Car Engine of the Future?" *Popular Science*, March 1989, 106.
86. Planet Watch (regular feature), "Fuel Changes Aren't Enough," *Consumer Reports*, January 1990, 14.
87. Estimate from the American Council for an Energy Efficient Economy, reported in *Popular Science*, October 1989, 53.
88. The Earthworks Group, *50 Simple Things You Can Do to Save the Earth* (Berkeley, Calif.: The Earthworks Press, 1989) 56-57.

Chapter 10

89. William K. Reilly, "A World in Our Hands," *The Washington Post*, 22 April 1990, B1.
90. William Booth and D'Vera Cohn, *The Washington Post*, 18 April 1990, A1.
91. Lester R. Brown et al., "A Global Plan to Save Our Planet's Environment," *USA Today* (Magazine), January 1990, 31.
92. The Earthworks Group. *50 Simple Things You Can Do to Save the Earth*, Berkeley, Calif.: The Earthworks Press, 1989, 56.
93. Jon Krakauer, "If You Want to Fight Air Pollution, Go Plant a Tree," *Smithsonian*, April 1990, 160.
94. CARE news release.
95. Quoted in Mickey Lemle, "New Horizons," *New Age Journal*, April 1990, 41.

BIBLIOGRAPHY

Books and Pamphlets

Abrahamson, Dean E., ed. *The Challenge of Global Warming.* Covelo, Calif.: Island Press, 1989.

Caplan, Ruth. *Our Earth, Ourselves.* New York: Bantam, 1989.

Cohen, Gary, and O'Connor, John, ed. *Fighting Toxics.* Covelo, Calif.: Island Press, 1990.

Council on Economic Priorities. *Shopping for a Better World.* New York: Ballantine Books, 1989.

Earthworks Group. *50 Simple Things You Can Do to Save the Earth.* Berkeley, Calif.: Earthworks Press, 1989.

Ehrlich, Paul, and Ehrlich, Anne. *The Population Explosion.* New York: Simon & Schuster, 1990.

Elkington, John; Hailes, Julia; and Makower, Joel. *The Green Consumer.* New York: Viking Penguin, 1990.

Gay, Kathlyn. *The Greenhouse Effect.* New York: Franklin Watts, 1986.

———. *Ozone.* New York: Franklin Watts, 1989.

———. *Silent Killers: Radon and Other Hazards.* New York: Franklin Watts, 1988.

Goldsmith, Edward, and Hildyard, Nicholas, ed. *The Earth Report: The Essential Guide to Global Ecological Issues.* Los Angeles: Price Stern Sloan, 1988.

Gribbin, John. *The Hole in the Sky.* New York: Bantam Books, 1988.

Heloise. *Hints for a Healthy Planet.* New York: Perigee, 1990.

Hunter, Linda Mason. *The Healthy Home.* Emmaus, Pa.: Rodale Press, 1989.

McDonald's Environmental Affairs. *McDonald's and the Environment* (pamphlet). Oak Brook, Ill.: McDonald's Corporation, 1990.

Regens, James L., and Rycroft, Robert W. *The Acid Rain Controversy.* Pittsburgh, Pa.: University of Pittsburgh Press, 1988.
Rifkin, Jeremy, ed. *The Green Lifestyle Handbook.* New York: Henry Holt, 1990.
Roan, Sharon. *Ozone Crisis.* New York: John Wiley & Sons, 1989.
Schneider, Stephen H. *Global Warming: Are We Entering the Greenhouse Century?* San Francisco: Sierra Club Books, 1989.
Steger, Will, and Bowermaster, Jon. *Saving the Earth: A Citizen's Guide to Environmental Action.* New York: Knopf, 1990.
U.S. Environmental Protection Agency. *Chemicals in Your Community: A Guide to the Emergency Planning and Community Right-to-Know Act.* Washington, D.C.: U.S. EPA, 1988.
Weiner, Jonathan. *The Next One Hundred Years: Shaping the Fate of Our Living Earth.* New York: Bantam Books, 1990.
Wild, Russell, ed. *The Earth Care Annual 1990.* Emmaus, Pa.: Rodale Press, 1990.

Periodicals

Abramson, Rudy. "Sleuths on the Trail of Weather." *Los Angeles Times*, 27 February 1990, A1.
"Air Conditioners That Won't Monkey with the Ozone Layer." *Business Week*, 25 April 1988, 131.
Allman, William F. "Rediscovering Planet Earth." *U.S. News & World Report*, 31 October 1989, 56-68.
Begley, Sharon. "Pollution Knows No Boundaries." *National Wildlife*, February/March 1990, 34-43.
Begley, Sharon, with Daniel Pedersen. "Fighting the Greenhouse." *Newsweek*, 18 June 1990, 51-52.
Bellafants, Ginia. "*Jogging Through the Smog.*" *Garbage*, July/August 1990, 52-56.
Booth, William. "Action Urged Against Global Warming: Scientist Appeal for Curbs on Gases." *Washington Post*, 2 February 1990, A4.
Booth, William, and Cohn, D'Vera. "Sharing the Environmental Burden: Many Americans Confused about How to Put Concern into Action." *The Washington Post*, 18 April 1990, A1.
Brown, Lester; Flavin, Christopher; and Postel, Sandra. "A Global Plan to Save Our Planet's Environment." *USA Today*, January 1990, 30.
Brundtland, Gro Harlem. "How to Secure Our Common Future." *Scientific American*, September 1989, 190.
Canine, Craig. "Home Energy." *Garbage*, November/December 1989, 20-27.
Carpi, John. "Metal Illnesses." *E. Magazine*, November/December 1990, 34-39.

Cherfas, Jeremy. "East Germany Struggles to Clean Its Air and Water." *Science*, 20 April 1990, 295-296.
Chiles, James R. "Tomorrow's Energy Today." *Audubon*, January 1990, 61-65.
"Earth: A User's Guide." *USA Today* 20, April 1990, Section E.
Easterbrook, Gregg. "Air Pollution: It's All Legal." *Newsweek*, 24 July 1989, 28-34.
Elmer-DeWitt, Philip. "A Drastic Plan to Banish Smog." *Time*, 27 March 1989, 65.
Erikson, Kai. "Toxic Reckoning: Business Faces a New Kind of Fear." *Harvard Business Review*, January-February 1990, 118-126.
Fisher, Arthur. "Global Warming." *Popular Science*, August 1989, 52-58; September 1989, 63-70; October 1989, 51-56, 92-98.
———. "Next Generation Nuclear Reactors: Dare We Build Them?" *Popular Science*, April 1990, 68-77.
Flavin, Christopher. "Slowing Global Warming." *American Forests*, May/June 1990, 37-44.
"The Fuels of the Future." *Consumer Reports*, January 1990, 11.
Gibbons, John H.; Blair, Peter D; and Gwin, Holly L. "Strategies for Energy Use." *Scientific American*, September 1989, 136-143.
Goldemberg, Jose. "How to Stop Global Warming." *Technology Review*, November/December 1990, 25-31.
"Golden Arches Join Global ReLeaf." *American Forests*, March/April 1990, 11.
Goodstein, Laurie. "An Awakening to Toxic Waste: Citizens Mobilize Against Longtime Chromium Hazard in New Jersey." *The Washington Post*, 17 September 1989, A3.
Gordon, Charles. "When the Heavens Turned Yellow." *Macleans*, 25 July 1988, 38.
Graedel, Thomas E., and Crutzen, Paul J. "The Changing Atmosphere." *Scientific American*, September 1989, 58-68.
Gray, Paul E. "We Need Safer Smaller Simpler Reactors." *Popular Science*, April 1990, 76.
Gray, Peter. "Will the Department of Energy Finally Stop Nuking America?" *The Washington Monthly*, April 1990, 38-46.
Hardin, Garrett. "Sheer Numbers: Can Environmentalists Grasp the Nettle of Population?" *E Magazine*, November/December 1990, 40-47.
Hirst, Eric. "Electricity: Getting More with Less." *Technology Review*, July 1990, 33-40.
Holmes, Hannah. "The States Set the Pace on Global-Warming Issues." *Garbage*, July/August 1990, 22-23.
Jager, Jill. "Anticipating Climate Change." *Environment*, September 1988, 13-15.

Jones, Philip D., and Wigley, Tom M. L. "Global Warming Trends." *Scientific American*, August 1990, 84–91.

Kalette, Denise, and Tyson, Rae. "Air: Treated Like an 'Open Sewer.'" *USA Today*, 31 July 1989, 5B.

Kenney, John. "Planet at the Crossroads." *National Parks*, March/April 1990, 24–28, 42–43.

Kerr, Richard A. "Global Warming Continues in 1989." *Science*, 2 February 1990, 521.

———. "Ozone Destruction Closer to Home." *Science*, 16 March 1990, 1297.

Keyfitz, Nathan. "The Growing Human Population." *Scientific American*, September 1989, 119–125.

Knox, Andrea. "Economist Looks Down the Line at Transit Subsidies." *Philadelphia Inquirer*, 26 February 1990, D3.

Krakauer, Jon. "If You Want to Fight Air Pollution, Go Plant a Tree." *Smithsonian*, April 1990, 160–171.

Leggett, Jeremy, and Stevenson, Peg. "Fiddling While the World Burns." *Greenpeace*, November/December 1990, 13–16.

Lemle, Mickey. "New Horizons." *New Age Journal*, March/April 1990, 38–43.

Lippman, Thomas W. "Bush Signs Sweeping Air Pollution Controls into Law." *The Washington Post*, 16 November 1990, A6.

Litweiler, John. "Allergic to Life." *Chicago Tribune*, 12 March 1990, Section 5, 1.

Mackenzie, James L., and El-Ashry, Mohamed T. Mohamed "Ill Winds: Air Pollution's Toll on Trees and Crops." *Technology Review*, April 1989, 65–71.

Makhijani, Arjun; Bickel, Amanda; and Makhijani, Annie, "'Beyond the Montreal Protocol: Still Working on the Ozone Hole." *Technology Review*, May/June 1990, 53–59.

———. "Plants for Healthier Homes." *Garbage*, March/April 1990, 36–43.

Mathews, Jessica T. "Coping with the Uncertainties of the Greenhouse Effect." *Harvard International Review*, Summer 1990, 10–12, 58–62.

McLoughlin, Merrill, with Betsy Carpenter, William J. Cook, and Andy Plattner. "Our Dirty Air." *U.S. News & World Report*, 12 June 1989, 48–54.

Merritt, Jim. "Outlook Variable." *Modern Maturity*, April–May 1990, 55–60.

Miller, Mark. "Trouble at Rocky Flats." *Newsweek*, 14 August 1989, 19–20.

Monastersky, Richard. "Cloudy Concerns." *Science News*, 12 August 1989, 106–110.

"Monitoring the Global Environment: An Assessment of Urban Air Quality." *Environment*, October 1989, 6-13;: 26-37.
Moore, Curtis A. "Will Changing Your Light Bulb Save the World?" *International Wildlife*, May/June 1989, 18-23.
Myers, Norman. "The Heat Is On: Global Warming Threatens the Natural World." *Greenpeace*, May/June 1989, 8-13.
Nadel, Brian. "Ozone-Friendly Cooling." *Popular Science*, July 1990, 57-59.
Nero, Anthony V., Jr. "Controlling Indoor Air Pollution." *Scientific American*, May 1988, 42-48.
Newton, James W., and Rohwedder, W. J. "Environmental Computer Networking." *E. Magazine*, March/April 1990, 45-47.
Nriagu, Jerome O. "Global Metal Pollution." *Environment*, September 1990, 7-11, 28-32.
Owen, Oliver S. "The Heat Is On: The Greenhouse Effect and the Earth's Future." *The Futurist*, September-October 1989, 34-40.
"Planet of the Year." *Time* (Special Issue), 2 January 1989.
Pollack, Stephanie. "Solving the Lead Dilemma." *Technology Review*, 22 October 1989, 22-31.
Poore, Patricia. "Clinical Ecology: Medicine for the Chemical-Sensitive?" *Garbage*, March/April 1990, 30-35.
Price, Martin F. "Global Change: Defining the Ill-Defined." *Environment*, October 1989, 18-20.
"Radon: The Problem No One Wants to Face." *Consumer Reports*, October 1989, 623-625.
Reiger, George. "Conservation Realities in the '90s." *American Forests*, March/April 1990, 17-19.
Riddle, Scott. "The Hidden Menace: Indoor Pollution." *USA Today* (Magazine), September 1989, 45.
Robinson, Eugene. "Brazil Finds Amazon's Fate Is Global Issue." *The Washington Post*, 26 February 1989, A29.
Ross, Philip E. "Clean-Air Fuels for the '90s." *Popular Science*, January 1990, 50.
Rothschild, Edwin S. "The Knock on High-Octane Gasoline." *The Washington Post*, 18 February 1990, B3.
Salby, Murry L., and Garcia, Rolando. "Dynamical Perturbations to the Ozone Layer." *Physics Today*, March 1990, 38-46.
"Say, Smokey: What's the Car Engine of the Future?" *Popular Science*, March 1989, 105-109.
Savage, Harlin. "Caution: The Air You Breathe May Be Hazardous to Your Health." *The National Voter*, June/July 1990, 4-9.
Schneider, Stephen H. "The Changing Climate." *Scientific American*, September 1989, 70-79.
Schoonmaker, David. "Are You Home Sick?" *Mother Earth News*, March/April 1989, 90-100.

Schulze, E. D. "Air Pollution and Forest Decline in a Spruce Forest." *Science*, 19, May 1989, 776–782.

Smith, Kirk. "Air Pollution: Assessing Total Exposure in the United States." *Environment*, October 1988, 10–15, 33–38.

Spencer, Roy W., and Christy, John R. "Precise Monitoring of Global Temperature Trends from Satellites." *Science*, 30 March 1990, 1558–1562.

Stammer, Larry B. "Indoor Air—How Clean Is It?" *The Washington Post*, 23 January 1990, Z17.

Stauffer, Nancy. "New Predictions on Ozone Pollution." *Technology Review*, November/December 1990, 13–14.

Steinhart, Peter. "Replanting the Forest." *Audubon*, March 1990, 26–29.

Stone, Pat. "Mother's Trees." *Mother Earth News*, March/April 1990, 108–112.

Stover, Dawn. "Refrigerators That Stay Cool Without CFCs." *Popular Science*, July 1990, 63, 90.

Stranahan, Susan Q. "It's Enough to Make You Sick." *National Wildlife*, February/March 1990, 8–15.

Sun, Marjorie. "Emissions Trading Goes Global." *Science*, 2 February 1990, 520–521.

"Supergreenhouse." *Popular Science*, April 1990, 27.

Thomas, Rich, and Schwartz, John. "Big Stink over a New Law." *Newsweek*, 9 April 1990, 42.

Udall, James R. "Turning Down the Heat." *Sierra*, July/August 1989, 32.

"Waiting for the Sunrise." *The Economist*, 19 May 1990, 95–98.

Wang, Penelope. "It's Not Easy Being Green." *Money*, April 1990, 101–112.

Waters, Tom. "Ecoglasnost." *Discover*, April 1990, 51–53.

"We Fouled Our Nest." *Newsweek*, 22 January 1990, 66–69.

Weisskopf, Michael. "Administration Defends Resistance to Plan for Helping Third World Cut CFCs." *The Washington Post*, 10 May 1990, A21.

_____. "Hypersensitivity to Chemicals Called Rising Health Problem." *The Washington Post*, 10 February 1990, A2.

"A White House Chill on Global Warming." *Newsweek*, 13 November 1989, 47.

Wicks, George, and Bickford, Dennis. "Doing Something about High-Level Nuclear Waste." *Technology Review*, November/December 1989, 51–58.

Wirth, Timothy. "Hotter and Hotter in the Greenhouse." *The Washington Post*, 20 February 1990, A21.

Wright, Karen. "The Shape of Things to Go." *Scientific American*, May 1990, 92–101.

ORGANIZATIONS TO CONTACT

Acid Rain Foundation, 1630 Blackhawk Hills, St. Paul, MN 55122.

Air Pollution Control Association, P.O. Box 2861, Pittsburgh, PA 15230.

American Council for an Energy-Efficient Economy (ACEEE), 1001 Connecticut Avenue NW, Suite 535, Washington, DC 20036.

Chemical Manufacturers Association, 2501 M Street, NW, Washington, DC 20037.

Citizens Clearinghouse for Hazardous Waste, P.O. Box 926, Arlington, VA 22216.

Environmental Defense Fund, 257 Park Avenue South, New York, NY 10010.

Environmental Research Foundation, P.O. Box 3541, Princeton, NJ 08543-3541.

Friends of the Earth, 530 Seventh Street SE, Washington, DC 20003.

Global ReLeaf, The American Forestry Association, P.O. Box 2000, Washington, DC 20013.

Greenpeace, 1436 U Street NW, Washington, DC 20009.

Household Hazardous Waste Project, 901 South National Avenue, Box 108, Springfield, MO 65804.

Institute for Local Self-Reliance, 2425 18th Street NW, Washington, DC 20009.

National Appropriate Technology Assistance Service (NATAS), U.S. Department of Energy, P.O. Box 2525, Butte, MT 59702-2525.

National Arbor Day Foundation, Arbor Lodge 100, Nebraska City, NE 68410.

National Audubon Society, 950 Third Avenue, New York, NY 10022.

National Coalition Against Misuse of Pesticides (NCAMP), 530 7th Street SE, Washington, DC 20003.

National Toxics Campaign, 37 Temple Pl., 4th Floor, Boston, MA 02111.

National Wildlife Federation, 1400 16th Street NW, Washington, DC 20036-2266.

The Nature Conservancy, 1815 N. Lynn Street, Arlington, VA 22209.

Sierra Club, 730 Polk Street, San Francisco, CA 94109.

The Rainbow Action Network, 301 Broadway, Suite A, San Francisco, CA 94133.

U.S. Environmental Protection Agency, Public Information Center, Washington, DC 20460.

U.S. Public Interest Research Group (PIRG), 215 Pennsylvania Avenue SE, Washington, DC 20036.

Worldwatch Institute, 1776 Massachusetts Avenue NW, Washington, DC 20036.

World Wildlife Fund, 1250 24th Street NW, Washington, DC 20037.

Computer Networks

The following organizations are telecommunication systems that offer data and public information on the environment.

EarthNet, P.O. Box 330072, Kahului, Maui, HI 96733.

EcoNet, 3228 Sacramento Street, San Francisco, CA 94114.

EnviroNet, Greenpeace Action, Building E, Fort Mason, CA 94123.

National Geographic Society, Educational Services, Department 1001, Washington, DC 20077.

RACHEL, Environmental Research Foundation, P.O. Box 3541, Princeton, NJ 08543-3541.

TOXNET, Toxicology Information Program, National Library of Medicine, 8600 Rockville Pike, Bethesda, MD 20894.

INDEX

Acid rain, 7, 26-38, 124
Aerosol products, 56
Agent Orange, 74
Agricultural crops, 18-19, 34-36, 61, 72-73, 74
Air, 8-9, 12
  See also Indoor air
Air conditioners, 65-66
Algae, 33, 124
Alpha track detector, 91
Aluminum, 33
Anions, 28, 30
Arrhenius, Svante, 39
Asbestos, 93-95
Ashford, Nicholas A., 99-100
Austral spring, 56

Benzene, 22, 98, 101
Bhopal, toxic leak, 67
Bioact EC 7, 66
Biogenic sources, 15, 88
Birth defects, 68, 88, 98
Blood disease, 23
Blurred vision, 99

Bromine, 66
Brown Haze, 14
Bush, George, 48-49, 64, 83

Cancer, 12, 61, 68, 69, 74, 77, 81, 88, 93, 94, 98
Carbon, 90, 111
Carbon dioxide, 42-43, 51, 52-53, 105, 108, 118, 121, 124
Carbon monoxide, 10, 12, 19-20, 93, 101, 124
Carson, Rachel, 71
Carter, Jimmy, 105, 107
Chemical sensitivity, 100
Chemical soup, 90
Chernobyl, nuclear accident, 81
Children, 93, 95-96
Chlordane, 71
Chlorine, 55, 58, 66
Chlorine dioxide, 58, 60
Chlorine nitrate, 55
Chlorofluorocarbons (CFCs or Freons), 40, 43, 54, 55-57, 62-66, 108, 124

141

Chromium dust, 77–78
Citizen protests, 75–78
Clean air, 102–113
Clean Air Act, 12, 13, 21, 22, 36, 38, 64, 71, 75, 102
Clean Air Amendments, 12, 69
Clouds, 47
Coal-burning, 7, 52
Coal-fired power plants, 38
Confusion, 99
Controls on pollution, 12–13
Copper, 79
Cyanide, 67

DDT, 71
Desiccant, 65
Developing countries, 11
Dioxins, 74, 124
Dizziness, 99
Dust, 95–97

Earth Day, 75, 77, 104, 114, 122
Ehrlich, Paul, 104
Electrical power, 6, 22, 109
Electric cars, 22–23
Electrochemical sensors, 57
Elkington, John, 122
Emissions, hazardous, 78–79
Energy efficiency, 111–113
Energy sources, renewable, 108–111
Environmental illness, 98
Ethanol, 22, 23, 24
Eye disorders, 61

Farms, 72, 73, 74
Fatigue, 97–98, 99
Fertilizers, 43
Fission, 83
Flavin, Christopher, 42
Flue gas desulfurization, 38
Forests, 42, 105
Formaldehyde, 23, 24, 97–98, 101

Fossil fuels, 10, 11, 27, 42, 49–50, 51, 105, 108, 109
Fuel rods, 83

Gasoline, 22, 23, 112–113
Geothermal, 108, 109
Getting involved, 122–123
Geysers, 52
Gibbons, John, 52
Global concerns, 102–104
Global warming, 10, 39–53
Glucose, 42
Gore, Albert, 42
Gray, Paul, 87
"Green" consumer, 120–123
Greenhouse effect, 125
Greenhouse experiments, 18
Greenhouse gases, 42, 43, 45, 105
Greenhouse Theory, 39–40

Hailes, Julia, 122
Halley Bay, 56
Halons, 55, 63, 64
Hansen, James, 45
Harwell, Mark, 105
Hayes, Denis, 75, 104
Headaches, 97
Health hazards, 60–61
Health problems, 12–13, 18
Heart, 18, 20
Herbicides, 71, 125
"Hole", 57
Hot springs, 52
Household products, 97–100
Houseplants, 101
Hydrocarbons, 10, 22, 125
Hydrogen, 24, 55
Hydrogen chloride, 55
Hydrogen ions, 28, 30
Hydropower, 108

Ice cores, 43
Immune system, 60–61
Incinerators, 73–74

Indoor air, 89-101
Industrial revolution, 9
Integrated pest management (IPM), 72-73
Interglacial periods, 43
International agreements, 107-108
Ions, 28, 30
Irving, Patricia, 36

Lead, 10, 79
Leaded gasoline, 22
Lead-laced air, 95-97
Leukemia, 23
Light bulbs, 113, 115, 117
Limestone scrubbers, 110
Lipkis, Andy, 117
Love canal, 74
Lovins, Amory, 111

Makower, Joel, 122
Marine life, 61
Marshall, George C., 50
Meadows, Donella H., 50
Mercury, 10, 33, 79
Methane, 40, 43, 45
Methanol, 22, 23, 24
Methylene chloride, 98
Methyl isocynate, 67
Miller, Claudia S., 100
Molina, Mario J., 56
Motor vehicles, 15, 19, 21, 71, 112
MTBE (Methyl tertiary butyl ether), 22

Nagasaki, 87
Natural gas, 22, 23
Nausea, 97-98, 99
Neurological disorders, 68
New fuels, 22-24
NGV (natural gas vehicles), 23
Nitrogen, 8, 33, 40, 55, 58
Nitrogen dioxide, 60
Nitrogen oxide, 10, 12, 15, 21, 22, 27-28, 37, 101

Nitrous oxide, 40, 43
"Non-attainment" areas, 12
Nuclear power, 80-81, 108
Nuclear waste, 81-87
Nuclear weapons plants, 81-83

Oxides of nitrogen, 10
Oxygen, 8, 54
Ozone, 10, 15, 16, 22, 27, 34, 40, 54, 55, 59, 117
Ozone depletion, effects of, 60-62
Ozone hole, 57, 58
Ozone layer, 10, 54-66, 125

Particulates, 12, 125
Peat, 108, 110
Perchloroethylene, 71
Pesticides, 71-73, 100
Petroferm, 66
pH (potential Hydrogen), 28, 30, 32, 35, 125
Photochemical process, 55, 125
Photosynthesis, 19, 42, 125
Photovoltaic, 110
Plutonium, 84, 125
PM10, 20
Poisons in the air, 67-79
Polar stratospheric clouds (PSCs), 55, 59
Politics, acid rain, 36-38
Polycarbonate plastic, 91
Population issue, 104-107
Pregnant women, 93
Premature aging, skin, 61
Premature deaths, 13
Public transit systems, 24-25

RACHEL, data base, 76
Radiation, 80-81, 125
    how much is safe, 87-88
Radioactivity, 80-81, 87-88
    See also Nuclear waste
Radium, 89
Radon, 9, 89, 90-92, 101, 125

Rainfall, 30
Rapid heartbeat, 99
Reactive chlorine, 55
Reagan, Ronald, 37
Reilly, William, 64, 112, 114
Respiratory problems, 12, 18, 68, 97, 98, 99
Rifkin, Jeremy, 122
Rowland, F. Sherwood, 56
Ruffins, Paul, 75

Salt water, 48
Satellites, 57
Saving energy, 115–117
Schneider, Stephen, 46
Shellfish, 32
Sick building syndrome, 90
Sidestream smoke, 93
"Sinks", 42
Skin, premature aging, 61
Smog, 14–25, 62
Smog chamber, 17
Smog ozone, 10, 15, 18–19
Smokestacks, 7
Smoking, 8, 10, 92–93, 98
Soil, and acid rain, 31–33
Solar power, 108, 109, 110
Soybeans, 35
Spent fuel, 83–84
SPM (solid particulate matter), 9, 126
Squamous-cell carcinoma, 61
Stratosphere, 54–55, 126
Stratospheric ozone, 60
Sulfur, 98, 101, 110
Sulfur dioxide, 10–12, 27, 37, 38
Sulfuric acid, 31
Sullivan, Louis, 92

Sunbathing, 61
Sununu, John, 49, 64

"Tall stacks", 28
TCE, 98, 101
Temperature, 45–47, 48
Termite populations, 45
Thornton, Kathy, 122
Three Mile Island, 80–81
Torres, Joseph, 120
Toxic chemical inventory, 68–71
Toxic emissions, 69
Toxic pollutants, amount, 8
Toxic waste
    See Nuclear waste
Trees, 19, 26, 33–34, 117–120
Tritium, 84
Troposphere, 15

U-235, 83, 84, 86
Uranium, 89
Uranium isotope, 83
Urban air pollutants, controlling, 20–21
Urban air quality, 11–12
Urban League, 76
UV radiation, 55, 61–62

Volatile organic compounds (VOCs), 10, 15, 16, 21, 24, 97, 98, 101

Waste, 73–75
Water, and acid rain, 31–33
Watkins, James D., 83, 87
"Wet scrubbing", 38
White House, 36–37, 48–51
Wind power, 108, 109

Yunick, Henry "Smokey", 112

363.73
Gay

12130

Bethany Christian Schools Library
Goshen, Indiana

3 0000 00004917 5